Teacher's

RESOURCE

Portfolio

for Our Christian Heritage in Art

Kathryn L. Bell

Bob Jones University Press
Greenville, South Carolina 29614

Advisory Committee

Philip D. Smith, Ed.D., *Provost*

Emery Bopp, M.F.A., *Chairman Emeritus of the Division of Art*

Teacher's Resource Portfolio for
OUR CHRISTIAN HERITAGE IN ART

Kathryn L. Bell, M.A.

Project Editors	**Computer Formatting**
Elizabeth B. Berg	Peggy Hargis
Carla Vogt	**Photo Acquisition**
Designer	Drew Fields
John Nolan	

Pigma Micron is a registered trademark of the Sakura Color Products Corporation.

Rapidograph is a registered trademark of KOH-I-NOOR, Inc.

Spackle is a registered trademark of Muralo.

Styrofoam is a registered trademark of Dow Plastics.

Tombow is a registered trademark of American Tombow, Inc.

ISBN 1-57924-207-3

15 14 13 12 11 10 9 8 7 6 5 4 3

Contents

To Parents and Teachers

Years ago when the Lord first laid on my heart a desire to write a book of art lessons for secondary students, I knew very little about how to organize such a book. In the years since then, massive changes have taken place in the world of art and art education. The most recent event has been the passage of the Goals 2000: Educate America Act. In that act, for the first time, the arts were recognized as component parts of a balanced education, and goals were included that will help to shape art education for years to come. Ordinarily, I would question any set of goals drawn up by a national educational body, but in this case, the visual arts goals represent a significant improvement over the former system of educating students in the visual arts.

A brief explanation is in order. Progressive educators and psychologists teamed up in the early years of the twentieth century to assign a place for arts education in the public schools. Their theories ranged from using art as a means of teaching other subjects to art as a means of producing a psychologically adjusted student and society. Most of those theories used art as a means of accomplishing something that had nothing to do with art. The avant-garde, by contrast, wanted art to be valued as experience. They defined that experience as the excitement of creative activity and eliminated all academic pursuits from the art room. Since there were no academic values involved, written curricula were regarded as superfluous; without written curricula, art teachers were on their own. Every teacher had to be his own planner, developer of curriculum, purchaser, and teacher. That situation produced much variety in content and methodology as well as much experimentation without any objective way to measure its success. Such teaching gave art education a haphazard quality in which whatever the art teacher liked best was covered thoroughly, and whatever he disliked was neglected altogether. The main focus was on creative artwork, but frequently the student had no idea what, besides "originality," was being asked of him. Successful teachers managed to teach their students about the structure and techniques of art; however, few teachers helped students learn to evaluate what they made or taught the fascinating history of art. Today with the National Visual Arts Standards, an important foundation has been laid for correcting those problems.

The National Visual Arts Standards identify the following six content areas that a qualified program in visual arts should meet. Such a program should help students

1. Understand and apply media, techniques, and processes;
2. Use knowledge of structures and functions;
3. Choose and evaluate a range of subject matter, symbols, and ideas;
4. Understand the visual arts in relation to history and cultures;
5. Reflect upon and assess the characteristics and merits of their work and the work of others;
6. Make connections between visual arts and other disciplines ("National Visual Arts Standards," *NAEA News,* June, 1994). The course of study outlined in this book is designed to fulfill these standards.

The material in the book is based for the most part on works in the BJU Museum and Gallery, Inc. Each chapter focuses on one or more works of art and includes a variety of activities that grow out of the study of that work. Each lesson covers material about the artist and his methods of working, the historical background of the artist and the work, seeing and perceiving the work, understanding and evaluating the work, and a series of creative expression lessons that build on the material covered. Methods also include basic academic skills such as reading, describing, discussion and listening, writing, role-playing, math skills, reasoning, observing, and making associations between art and other knowledge. Ideally, to maintain the balance between academic knowledge and creative activity, the lessons should be used in their entirety. But it is also possible to teach the academic portions of the book as an "art appreciation" class. However, the results will be less satisfying since the vital connection between the study of art and the production of art will be lost. I strongly suggest teaching by the question/answer method because it encourages thought and expression on the part of the students. Do not allow the academic portions to become a monologue on the part of the teacher.

Perhaps I have gone too far without answering the basic question "Why should Christian teens study art in the first place?" Sometimes the assumption is made that only those who have a mysterious quality called talent should be allowed to study art. Certainly if God has given young people ability in art, they should be encouraged to develop it, but the study of art has benefits for other students as well.

1. The study of art teaches them to recognize and value quality both in art and in life. The great majority of our decisions are based on perceived quality. For every wrong thing, there is another that is acceptable, another that is better, and still another that is best. The Word of God tells us to value what is excellent.

2. The process of art-making helps students to understand the creative process and encourages understanding of others as they share their personal creations with each other.

3. Art-making stimulates imagination by asking the students to plan, revise, innovate, and finish a project. Seeing other students working on the same project and designing very different solutions to a common problem develops flexibility of thinking.

4. Involvement in complex tasks requires commitment on the part of the student to persevere and finish.

5. Learning to evaluate their own and others' work develops the students' skills for analyzing, evaluating, observing, and reasoning. These judgmental skills make them visually literate people who can defend their opinions with facts. Students learn to make judgments based not only on visual skills but also on scriptural knowledge. Biblical principles are applied to a variety of situations.

6. The study of art in relation to the history of its time gives history a human face and form. At the same time, the study of history helps us to interpret what the artist has portrayed. The political, religious, economic, and intellectual climate of an age has a profound influence on the art of that age (basic concepts from *Academic Preparation in the Arts*, College Entrance Examination Board, 1985).

Each of these skills is a useful addition to the education of young adults in all areas of life. Our age is growing increasingly visual in its communication. Christians who understand the purpose and the strengths and weaknesses of the visual arts are not only better prepared to use their gifts to bring glory to God, but they are also better equipped to discern the moral and artistic implications of any message communicated in a visual way. Let us not abandon, but reclaim and preserve our rich Christian heritage in art.

Note: Several maps are included in the margin of the student text. The purpose of these maps varies. In some instances, they are intended to clarify detailed historical information. In other cases, they merely serve to give the student a sense of place, a broad overview of where specific artists were born or artistic movements originated. The amount of detail as well as the choice of geographic information was dependent on the intended purpose. Understanding this approach may help you in determining how best to use each map for your classroom setting.

Introduction: The Tabernacle

To introduce the students to their Christian heritage in art, have them complete the Studies of the Tabernacle worksheet (reproducible) on pages 65-69 of this Resource Portfolio. This exercise will lay the foundation for subsequent lessons, enabling students to see how the study of art can serve the purpose of Christian education—to conform redeemed man to the image of God. God is the author of beauty, and our desire to create beauty is a reflection of His image in us.

In the study of the tabernacle in the Old Testament, we have an excellent opportunity to see God's aesthetic principles at work, "that this material dwelling-place of God might be a safe guide and real assistance in promoting fellowship with Heaven—that it might convey only right impressions of divine things, and form a suitable channel of communication between God and man—it must evidently be constructed so as to express God's ideas, not man's" ("The Tabernacle in Its General Structure," *ISBE*, p. 204). This aim was uniquely accomplished, for the form and specific details of the construction and decoration were given by God to Moses just as His Word was given (Exod. 25:8-9). Furthermore, the craftsman in charge of the project, Bezaleel, was filled with the Holy Spirit. What we are looking at, therefore, is not the art of man, but the art of God. Among the many lessons that can be learned from a study of the tabernacle is a lesson on the proper use of art for God's glory.

Studies of the Tabernacle: Art for God's Glory

I. The Nature of God

1. Read Genesis 1:26-27. What does it tell us about ourselves? *(We are created in God's image.)*
2. In Genesis 1:29-30, God explains to Adam why He put so many plants in the Garden of Eden. What reason does He give? *(to provide food for man and animals)* In Genesis 2:9 He adds a different reason. What is it? *(They were pleasant to the sight.)* What does this second reason show us about God? *(He appreciates beauty.)* What does this knowledge about God show us about ourselves? *(Because we are made in His image, we are able to appreciate beauty too.)*
3. Read Psalm 19:1-4. What is the language that goes out to all the earth? *(line)* According to this passage, this language has no words that can be heard. You can easily see this if you read the verse without the italicized words. It says, "No speech nor language; their voice is not heard."

4. In Psalm 8:3-4 we learn what the silent language of the heavens is teaching. What is it? *(how little we are compared to the universe)*
5. When God was giving the instructions for the building of the tabernacle and its furnishings, He instructed the seamstresses who sewed the garments for Aaron and his sons to put pomegranates and bells along the hem of the garment. He gave two reasons. What were they (Exod. 28:2, 40)? *(glory and beauty)*
6. What does the example of the lily in Matthew 6:28-30 show us about the beauty of things in nature? *(It is much better than anything that man can make.)* Even the tiny creatures that live in the deepest, remotest parts of the sea exhibit great beauty. Because men cannot travel to those depths, they must send machines down to photograph the animals that live there. Those organisms carry their own powerful floodlights to illuminate their world since no sunlight penetrates that far. They live in darkness, unseen by the human eye, yet they are very beautiful. For whom was their beauty created? *(for God Himself)*

II. The Artist

1. Read Exodus 20:4-6. The first thing God says about art is negative. What is it that God is prohibiting in this commandment? *(making images to worship)* Now read Exodus 25:10, 18-20. Which of the furnishings of the tabernacle is being described? *(the ark of the covenant)* What is to be placed on each side of it? *(carved cherubim with their wings over the ark)* From these verses what can we conclude about art? *(Sculpture itself is not forbidden, even in a place of worship. God forbids the worship of an object made by man.)* Remember that the Israelites had lived for four hundred years in Egypt where they saw idols worshiped every day. Many of them were probably involved in idol worship themselves.
2. In Exodus 31:2-11 two men were chosen. What are their names? *(Bezaleel and Aholiab)* How did God prepare them for their job? *(He filled Bezaleel with His Spirit, and He gave both Bezaleel and Aholiab wisdom.)* List the specific things they were going to do for God. *(design skillful work; work in gold, silver, and bronze; cut and set stones; carve wood; make the tabernacle, its furnishings, the clothes for the priests, and oil for incense)* In Exodus 35:34 what else had God called them to do? *(teach others)* List the other workers who were to be filled with wisdom (v. 35). *(engraver, skillful workman, embroiderer, weaver, de-*

signer) In Exodus 28:3 another group is mentioned. What were they to make? *(Aaron's priestly garments)*

3. Proverbs 10:16 tells us what the result of our labors will be. Read Proverbs 31:13, 18-19, 21-22, 24. How is this lady a good example of labor that tends to life? *(She works willingly with her hands; her work is good; she works into the night; she weaves; she provides for her family; she makes beautiful things for herself as well; she sells her work.)*

4. Ephesians 4:28 tells us another reason that we should labor. What is it? *(so that we can have something to give to others)* Is the woman in Proverbs 31 an example of this also? *(yes)*

5. Philippians 4:8-9 tells us to focus our thoughts on things that please the Lord. If our thoughts are right, our actions will be also. List all the words in this passage that describe what we must think about. *(true, honest, just, pure, lovely, of good report, virtuous, praiseworthy)*

6. How will our artwork be judged before Christ someday? That depends on what we do and how we do it. Look at I Corinthians 3:12-15. Since the work is to be tested by fire, why should we want to be using gold or silver instead of wood, hay, or stubble? *(Gold and silver are better after the fire purifies them; wood, hay, and stubble are destroyed by fire.)*

7. The gold, silver, wood, hay, and stubble are metaphors, words that stand for something else. What do you think might be the things God wants to see in a Christian artist? *(Students will suggest various things, but those should include the things found in Proverbs 31 and in Philippians 4:8-9.)*

III. The Materials and Methods Used

1. In Exodus 35:5-9 Moses told the people what was needed in order to build the tabernacle. List the things they contributed. *(gold; silver; brass; blue, purple, and scarlet linen; goats' hair; rams' skins dyed red; badgers' skins; shittim wood; oil; spices; onyx stones; and other precious stones)*

2. Did they contribute enough (Exod. 36:5-6)? *(yes, more than enough)*

3. Where did the former slaves get so much gold (Exod. 35:22 and 11:2-3)? *(from jewelry; by asking the Egyptians for it just before they left Egypt)*

4. What is the "blue, and purple, and scarlet" that the people were to bring (Exod. 35:6, 25)? *(dyed linen yarn)* What is "goats' hair"? *(yarn from goat hair)*

Did you know that cashmere, which is used to knit very soft sweaters, is made from the long wool of a goat?

The "badgers' skins" in verse 7 could be translated "seal skins" or "porpoise skins." These skins would make a waterproof covering. The "shittim wood" in the same verse is

acacia wood. Acacia wood is available in that part of the world and is a very durable, hard wood that was used for building boats.

5. What kind of oil was going to be used for burning the lamps (Exod. 27:20)? *(pure olive oil)* Who brought the oil and spices (Exod. 35:27-28)? *(rulers)* Why do you suppose *they* specifically were asked to bring these things? *(Perhaps they were wealthier than the other Israelites and could afford these things.)*

6. What kinds of stones were brought for the ephod (Exod. 39:10-13)? *(sardius, topaz, carbuncle, emerald, sapphire, diamond, jacinth (ligure), agate, and amethyst)*

7. Why did the people give (Exod. 35:21-22)? *(Their hearts were stirred; they willingly gave.)*

8. In chapters 35-39, several artistic processes are listed. What are they? *(spinning yarn [Exod. 35:25]; cutting and setting stones [Exod. 35:33]; engraving, embroidery, and weaving [Exod. 35:35]; gold overlay [Exod. 36:34]; casting metal [Exod. 37:13]; beating gold [Exod. 37:17]; making incense and anointing oil [Exod. 37:29]; making garments [Exod. 39:1])*

9. What did the engraver engrave (Exod. 39:6)? *(onyx stone)*

10. What decoration was embroidered on the hem of the holy garments that were made for Aaron and his sons (Exod. 28:33)? *(blue, purple, or scarlet pomegranates)*

Pomegranates are red, not blue or purple. Many of the decorations in the tabernacle were nonrealistic. The *Zondervan Pictorial Encyclopedia of the Bible* states that pomegranates may symbolize the unity of God's Word composed of many separate parts. The inside of a pomegranate contains many small, sweet, berrylike fruits. The pomegranate was one of the fruits gathered by the spies to show the wonderful fruit that grew in Israel (Num. 13:23).

IV. The Tabernacle as a Symbol

1. What was the purpose of the tabernacle (Exod. 29:45-46)? *(to help Israel remember God's goodness to them)*

2. Where was the tabernacle to be located (Num. 1:53; 2:17)? (Check Num. 2:3, 10, or 18-25.) *(in the middle of all the tribes)*

3. In Hebrews 9:24, the Bible says the things in the Old Testament were "figures of the true" things in heaven. Each of the parts of the tabernacle is a picture of the truth of redemption. What objects were found in the outer court of the tabernacle (Exod. 40:6-8)? *(altar of burnt offering, laver)* What was the bronze altar used for (Exod. 40:29)? *(burnt offerings)* What is the meaning of this activity for us (Heb. 9:25-26)? *(It was a type of Christ's death for our sin.)* What was the laver used for (Exod. 30:18-21)? *(washing the priests' hands*

and feet before the priests entered the tabernacle) What does the washing of the priests mean to us (John 13:9-10)? *(It symbolizes Christ's atonement for our sins—i.e., His cleansing, or renewing, of our nature by His sacrifice.)* The verses in Exodus 30 show Christians the seriousness of keeping their lives free from sin.

4. What furnishings were found inside the tabernacle but not in the holy of holies (Exod. 40:22-26)? *(table, lampstand, and golden altar)* What was put on the table (Lev. 24:5-7)? *(loaves of bread with frankincense on them)* Why were there twelve? *(the twelve tribes of Israel)* According to Leviticus 24:2-3, when was the lampstand burned? *(all the time)* What does the light reveal (II Cor. 4:6)? *(the knowledge of the glory of God)* What was the little altar used for (Exod. 30:7-8)? *(for burning incense in the morning and evening)* According to Psalm 141:2, what does incense symbolize? *(prayer)*

5. Inside the tabernacle, behind the veil, there was only one object. What was it (Exod. 40:2-3)? *(the ark of the testimony)* What was the "mercy seat" (Exod. 25:22)? *(God's throne—the place from which He communed with the priest)* What beings were sculpted on it (v. 19)? *(cherubim—one on each side)* Where do these beings serve (Ezek. 10:19-20)? *(before the door of the Lord's house, below God's glory)* Once a year, the high priest entered the holy of holies. What did he do there (Lev. 16:14-15)? *(He sprinkled the blood of the sacrifice on the mercy seat.)* What does the sacrifice of the high priest picture for us (Heb. 9:12)? *(Christ's entering the holy place with His own blood to redeem us)*

6. Once the beautiful objects were finished and put into the tabernacle, what happened (Exod. 40:34-35, 38)? *(The glory of the Lord filled it.)* How many people could enter the holy place of the tabernacle (Lev. 16:17)? *(one)* Could the ark of the covenant be seen? *(no)* Why (Lev. 16:11-13)? *(The incense that was offered made a cloud that hid the ark.)* Could it be seen when it was moved (Num. 4:15, 20)? *(No. It was covered with the veil by Aaron, the high priest; nobody else was allowed to see it.)*

In Hebrews 9, God reveals the symbolism of the tabernacle: it is to show us how to worship God. First of all, our sin had to be paid for with a death (the bronze altar/the cross); then our daily sins must be cleansed (the laver/confession, I John 1:9). When we enter God's presence (the tabernacle), we want Him to remember us (the loaves of showbread), we need light to see His glory (the lampstand), and we must pray (the altar of incense). Only then can we appear in God's presence (before the mercy seat) and find "grace to help in time of need" (Heb. 4:16).

Bibliography

Caldecott, W. Shaw. "Tabernacle." *International Standard Bible Encyclopedia.* 5 vols. Edited by James Orr. Grand Rapids, Mich.: William B. Eerdmans Publishing Co., 1939.

Moorehead, W. G. *The Tabernacle, The Priesthood, Sacrifices and Feasts of Ancient Israel.* Grand Rapids, Mich.: Kregel Publications, 1957.

Chapter 1: Mosaics: the Visual Bible

Additional Historical Information on the Religious Climate During the Church Age

Nearly everything we know concerning religion during the Middle Ages comes from Roman Catholic or Greek Orthodox sources. Consequently, just about every "Christian" from A.D. 500 to 1500 was a "Catholic." This does not mean, however, that there were no true believers in this period or that all true believers were living in disobedience. The religious situation in those days was quite different. First, biblical knowledge was not as widespread then as it is now. Few of the commoners could read, and those who were educated rarely even saw a Bible. Their understanding came almost exclusively through the preaching they received. Therefore, wherever there was a converted clergyman, there could have been many believers who possessed a biblical understanding of the gospel; however, because of a lack of scriptural knowledge, they did not correctly perceive many of its important implications (just as anyone who receives the Lord but is not properly discipled). Second, it should not surprise us that believing clergy did not leave the church, because such a drastic move would have seemed an impossibility. Both the Greek Orthodox and Roman churches were as broad as European society itself. To leave the organized church would have meant leaving civilization. Third, the doctrinal imprecision of Roman Catholicism and the Greek Orthodox Church during this period allowed true believers to live within the organized church without fear of offending their consciences. Exactly what Rome believed about justification by faith was not clearly enunciated until the reformers forced the issue. The first specific, authoritative statement on this critical point came at the Council of Trent (1545-63). The fact that thousands did leave the church once these doctrinal lines were drawn seems to indicate that many throughout the Middle Ages believed in justification by faith alone.

The modern religious situation, however, is indeed different. Because of the work of the reformers and the Council of Trent, the teaching of the Roman Catholic Church is very clear. Because of the accessibility of the Scriptures and their interpretation, communicants within the church no longer have an excuse for being biblically ignorant. Though it is still possible for a believer to remain in the Roman Catholic Church, to do so he must be inexcusably ignorant of the Scripture or the teaching of the church, or he must be willfully living in disobedience to God's Word.

Seeing and Perceiving (p. 16)

Questions and Answers

The Parting of Abraham and Lot

1. The composition is divided into two almost equal sections. What kind of balance is this? *(symmetrical)*
2. Which of the figures represents Lot? Which represents Abraham? *(Lot is on the right; Abraham is on the left.)*
3. How can you tell? *(You can tell by the number of children; larger buildings indicate a city; there is a tree on Abraham's side.)*
4. How does the artist show the robes and how they fold? *(He does so by using different values of color to shade them.)*
5. How far away is the most distant object in the picture? *(The most distant object looks as if it is directly behind the figures.)*
6. What can you see in the mosaic that shows a conventional representation? *(You can see the small houses, which symbolize Sodom; the tabernacle and tree, which symbolize countryside; and the group of heads behind Abraham and Lot, which symbolize families.)*

Understanding and Evaluating (p. 17)

Questions and Answers

1. Read Genesis 13:6-12. What do you think is the emotional climate of this family at this time? *(Students will have differing opinions here, depending on their own experiences of family conflict. This may be an opportune time to distinguish biblical principles from personal pride.)*
2. Did the artist see the emotional climate the same way you did? How did he represent the emotions of the people in the family? *(He represented the emotions of the people by showing them leaning or tilting their heads or by the gestures of their arms.)*
3. What does Lot's gesture communicate to you? *(His gesture seems closed, perhaps indicating a turning away, a pushing away of his family.)*
4. What about Abraham's gesture? *(Abraham's gesture is more open, seemingly including Lot in the family; Abraham's gesture may indicate a continued willingness to negotiate, perhaps a hesitation to separate.)*
5. Do the wives and children seem to have any say in the decision? *(No. They seem to be following the two fathers.)*

Creative Expression Lessons

Lesson one: Designing a symbol

Materials needed
- newsprint, 9" × 12"
- pencils
- chalk or tracing paper
- black construction paper, 9" × 12"
- scissors
- glue sticks or paper glue
- white drawing paper, 9" × 12"

Objectives
The students will do the following:
- Choose an abstract idea and a simple shape to represent that idea
- Cut out the symbolic shape and mount it

Procedure (pp. 17-18)
1. In class discussion, list several simple shapes that are symbols. They may include a red hexagonal shape for "stop" or a circle for eternity.
2. Choose from the list those that symbolize ideas that are abstract, like "eternity." Add other words to the list of abstract ideas. Avoid obvious ideas.
3. Choose a simple shape that can represent that idea.
4. Draw the shape as a silhouette. Include only as many details as are necessary to identify what it is. Trace the shape on a piece of black paper and cut it out with scissors. Glue it to a sheet of white paper and write the idea on the back.

Assessments
- Hang finished work on a bulletin board and have the students try to name the idea behind each person's symbolic shape.
- Evaluate the students' work for idea, symbolism, and careful workmanship.

Lesson two: Beginning mosaic

Materials needed
- students' own Bibles
- heavy poster board or mat board (foam board will also work)
- pencils
- wax crayons
- various colors of construction paper
- old electric iron (optional)
- waxed paper
- scissors
- watercolor paints (optional)
- white glue diluted with water (1:1) in small jars
- old craft brushes
- acrylic gesso or acrylic paint
- old or inexpensive house painting brushes

Objectives
The students will do the following:
- Design a simple illustration based on a Bible story of their choice
- Complete the illustration with paper mosaic

Procedure (p. 18)
1. Use your Bible to find a story. Read it and decide which specific incident you want to illustrate.
2. It may be helpful to act out the story in order to determine what gestures will express the story best. For this reason, your teacher may have you work as a group on this project.
3. Sketch the characters with pencil on poster board, using light lines. Make figures big enough to avoid details that will be impossible to make with mosaics. Fill the whole area with your sketch. Use frontal views of figures and large gestures to convey the action. Scenery or other props should be included if they will help to tell the story.
4. Using construction paper and wax crayons, make the mosaic tiles. Color heavily on the paper, using a variety of closely related colors. Tile can be solid colored or streaky, dotted or patterned with the crayon. Make tiles of all the colors you will need for your mosaic. If you want to blend the colors further, iron over them with a warm iron. Use a piece of waxed paper over the crayon to protect the iron. Cut your tile into small individual squares measuring approximately ½ to 1 centimeter square.
5. With your teacher's permission, you may use watercolors to paint in the illustration as the mosaicists did, or you may leave the poster board white. Gray poster board will reduce the contrast of the white paper with the mosaic tiles.
6. Spread diluted white glue over a small portion of the poster board and begin adhering your tiles to it. They should be very close together so that hardly any of the background paper shows through. Cut pieces to fit the spaces. Be sure to make shapes contrast with backgrounds in color and value so that they can easily be seen.

7. When you have glued some tile on, you will find the poster board curling up. To correct that, turn it face-down and paint the back with white acrylic gesso or acrylic paint.

Assessments
- Have the students exchange sketches and try to guess what is being illustrated. Have the class evaluate their

own and/or each other's work for effective communication of the story.

- Evaluate the finished mosaic for clarity of communication, contrast of color, and simplicity of shapes.

Lesson three: Drawing an editorial cartoon

Materials needed
- editorial cartoons
- newspapers and magazines
- Bible concordance
- newsprint
- pencils
- white drawing paper

Teacher's choice of the following:
- India ink (black, non-waterproof)
- variety of drawing pen nibs
- pen staffs or various thicknesses of Rapidograph drawing pens or Pigma Micron pens (black)

Objectives
The students will do the following:
- Examine editorial cartoons and discuss the issues being communicated
- Research an issue and make an editorial cartoon to communicate the issue

Procedure (pp. 18-19)
1. Bring editorial cartoons to class and hang them on the bulletin board.
2. Examine several cartoons and see if you can identify the point of view of the artist. What is his solution to the problem? Does he just make fun of others' solutions?
3. Choose a controversial issue in your local community.
4. Using newspapers, magazines, and perhaps radio talk shows, gather arguments on both sides of the issue.
5. Use a Bible concordance to find the verses that address the issue. Determine your position by following what the Bible says and backing it up with the facts you found in your research. You may write a short report on your position.
6. Plan your cartoon with sketches. Determine what kinds of figures to use and what actions they should be doing. Do many sketches.
7. Trace the best details of your sketches lightly in pencil and go over them in ink. Use thicker pens for major outlines and for filling in areas with black; use thinner pens for details and shading.

Assessments
- Guide students in their choice and research of a controversial issue, making sure that they have evaluated the issue in light of biblical principles and that this evaluation is clear in what they communicate in their drawing.
- Observe students to determine their understanding of the position of editorial cartoonists and what they communicate.

Chapter 2: *Patrick and the Irish Monastic Movement*

Seeing and Perceiving (pp. 25-27)

Questions and Answers

1. Look at the incipit page carefully. How many colors do you see? *(There are about six colors: red, blue, green, ocher, lavender, black, and perhaps a little white.)*

2. Do you see any animals? *(There are birds and what looks like a cat on the right side.)*

3. What other shapes do you see? *(There are interlaced lines, spirals, and dots.)*

4. Can you find examples of each of these motifs on the page? *(An example of interlaced lines can be seen in the patterns in the letter* q *and in the filling in the space at the left. The birds in the area at the left side also show the interlacing of lines [the animals]. Spirals are seen at the ends of the* q *and in the animal whose body makes a spiral. Notice the hind legs and tail of the catlike animal; its head is at the lower right, and its hind legs are at the top of the page above the* u.)

5. How could Eadfrith have made such neat spirals and straight lines? *(He used a ruler and compass to draw the shapes.)*

6. Can you find the symbol that is used for *M* in the second word? *(It looks like a telephone pole.)* The next word ends with three strange shapes that represent the letters *o, n,* and *a.*

7. Why do you think Eadfrith used these forms instead of the more normal ones he used in other words? *(He had to change sizes and forms to fit the word into the space before the border; he also carried word parts over to the next line to make lines come out evenly.)*

8. Eadfrith decorated the letters as well as the border. How many different kinds of ornamentation did he use in and between letters? *(Five; he used pebble-fill dots, diamond patterns, interlaced dots, interlaced lines, and solid colors.)*

9. Looking at the style of decoration, why do you think the scribes might have made these changes in the alphabet? *(They liked things that were a little irregular or unusual in shape, and they liked things that connected [interlaced lines].)*

10. Examine the page of calligraphic writing from the Lindisfarne Gospels. At what angle was the pen touching the paper? *(Its edge was touching the parchment almost horizontally.)*

11. How can you tell? *(All the thin lines and flat ends of strokes line up on the horizontal.)*

12. Letters begin with large triangular-shaped serifs. If the pen is being held flat, how would these serifs have to be made? *(They would have to be made by having two lines overlapping each other.)*

13. How does Eadfrith change the shape of *e* and *c* compared with *o*? *(Usually we think of all these letters as circular, but he has made some of his letters noncircular.)*

14. Why do you think he did that? *(He did it so that the letter could be connected to the next letter at the bottom.)*

Understanding and Evaluating (p. 28)

Questions and Answers

1. The decoration—especially on incipit pages—was integral to the text. Which do you think may have been more important to the scribes, the decoration or the words? *(the decoration)*

2. What makes you think that? *(The carelessness about errors of text and the carefulness in decorating the page seem to confirm the point.)*

Creative Expression Lessons

Lesson one: Writing Irish majuscule

Materials needed
- alphabet charts
- wide-ruled notebook paper for practice
- pencils
- chisel-edged, water-based marker
- ruler with metric (2 mm) markings
- white drawing paper
- Bible

Objectives
The students will do the following:
- Learn to write the Irish majuscule alphabet
- Letter a Bible verse in Irish majuscule

Procedure (pp. 29-30)
1. Copy the forms of the letters from the chart using a pencil and drawing a single line for each letter. Pay special attention to the shape of each part of the letter and the proportion of its width to its height.

proportions too narrow   proportions correct

2. When you have become familiar with the letter shapes, use them to write sentences. Remember that

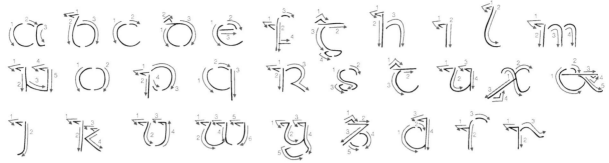

letters added later to write foreign languages   alternate forms of *d, s, r*

a bcdefghilmu
opqrstux &
jkvwyz dfr
cai ct ct ft o lu tai

the Irish scribes connected letters as often as possible, except between words.

3. Using a chisel-edged marking pen that has an edge about two millimeters wide, practice making shapes. Hold the pen so that its wide edge touches the paper all the way across and so that the flat edge is horizontal. Practice the kinds of shapes you see in the Irish majuscule letters: triangular serifs, round and out-of-round shapes, and straight stems.

4. Practice the Irish majuscule letters using the chisel-edged marker. Use guidelines that are eight millimeters apart.

5. Write out a Bible verse. Leave a space between lines that equals the height of the letters. If you are going to do Lesson three, omit the first letter of the verse.

Assessments
- Guide the students in their evaluations of the letter shapes and proportions.
- Have each student evaluate the final copy for consistent letter form.

Lesson two: Designing illumination

Materials needed
- white drawing paper
- medium-hard pencils such as HB or H
- erasers
- rulers
- Pigma Micron pen (black) or Rapidograph pen with black ink
- photocopier
- scissors
- transparent tape
- colored pencils (soft, waxy type)

Objectives
The students will do the following:
- Design an illuminated border
- Plan colors to use in the border

Procedure (p. 30)
1. Draw several "ribbons" that cross each other at right angles. Make them interlace by erasing the one that goes underneath. Ribbons should alternate between going over, then under, then over again. Connect the ends so that the entire design is one or two complete shapes. Keep the ribbons in a square or rectangular arrangement. Surround them with a frame of straight lines.

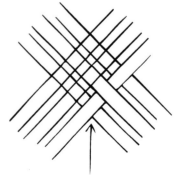

2. Trace over your finished design with ink or fine-point marker pen. Make four or more copies on a photocopier. Cut them out and tape them together end to end so that they make one long border. Make two copies of the taped-together border design.

3. Color them with colored pencils. Pick out one color for the background and another for the interlace. You may want to color one ribbon a different color from the other to make them more distinct. You may also reverse colors each time the design repeats. Display the trial copies so that the class can look at all of them together. Evaluate the effectiveness of the colors chosen.

4. If the design is too large, reduce its size on the copier until the design looks right with the letters. Trace the design onto the paper to make a border for the verse you lettered. If you are going to do Lesson three, wait until then to trace the border onto the paper.

5. Color the good copy with the colors you liked best in your trial copy.

Assessment
- Guide the class in evaluating their colors and designs.

Lesson three: Designing a large capital letter to go with the border and verse

Materials needed
- white drawing paper
- pencils
- Pigma Micron pen (black) or Rapidograph pen with black ink
- colored pencils (soft, waxy type)
- gold paint marker, fine point (optional)

Objectives
The students will do the following:
- Draw an enlarged letter and then color and decorate it
- Include the letter along with the illuminated border on their verse

Procedure (pp. 30-31)
1. Choose a form for your initial letter from those on the incipit page or enlarge a normal letter from the Irish majuscule alphabet. If your verse starts with "and," you may use the ampersand. Draw the chosen letter

as high as two lines of writing with their space in between. Outline it with pencil; do not write it with the marker.

ampersand

2. Choose a decorative motif to use in the space inside the letter. Draw it lightly.

3. You may wish to write the letter in solid black, or you may outline it with a solid color and put designs inside the strokes.

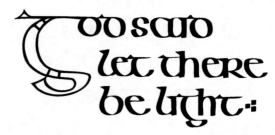

4. Decorate the outside of the letter strokes with outlines or dots. Go over all outlines and decorations with the fine-point black pen.

5. Choose colors that repeat those used on the border and color in the decorations you designed.

6. Determine how your letter will relate to the ends of the border you designed. The border and the letter should be separate.

7. Trace the letter and border onto the verse you lettered and color the designs.

Assessments
- Guide the class in evaluating the finished work: quality and consistency of lettering, design, and first letter.
- Evaluate the finished work for consistency of lettering, choice of colors and design of illumination, and unity of total effect.

Chapter 3: *Patterns of Infinity: Islamic Decoration*

Seeing and Perceiving (p. 36)

Questions and Answers

1. How many different patterns can you count on the wall of the Dome of the Rock? *(Answers will vary.)*
2. How did the artisans distinguish these patterns from each other? *(They distinguished them by framing them in straight lines as well as by reversing color patterns or changing patterns or sizes of patterns.)*
3. What effect does this use of pattern have on the appearance of the wall? Does the wall look massive, or does it look light in weight? *(Students' opinions may vary; most experts say it looks light—almost immaterial because of the pattern.)*

Understanding and Evaluating (p. 37)

Questions and Answers

1. Do these abstract designs mean something more than mere decoration? Can you guess what these decorations might mean? *(They may be symbols of the order of the universe—symbols for God, man, and the universe.)*
2. Do you remember how these passages are reconciled in our study of the tabernacle? *(Exodus 20:4-5 and 25:18-20 can be reconciled when we discern that it is not the making of images but the worship of images that is sinful.)*

Creative Expression Lessons

Lesson one: Tile designs that connect

Materials needed
- white drawing paper
- rulers
- pencils
- copier
- transparent tape
- colored pencils
- fine-point, water-based colored markers

Objectives
The students will do the following:
- Make a single tile design
- Integrate the design into one new, larger design
- Color the design using a limited color scheme and repeating colors in regular patterns

Procedure (p. 38)
1. Draw a twelve-inch square on a piece of paper. Using a ruler, divide each of the sides into equal one-inch sections.
2. Beginning in the corner or the middle of one side, draw a shape inside a small area of the square. Draw the same shape in each corresponding area (i.e., each of the other corners or the middle of the other three sides, depending on where you started).
3. Continue to draw shapes in other areas, remembering to repeat them in all the corresponding areas. The shapes should have a similar nature (i.e., geometric shapes or natural shapes, angular shapes or rounded ones).
4. Continue to work in toward the center of the square.
5. Some areas may be filled in with black or with patterns, as long as they follow the symmetry of the whole design.
6. Make four copies of the design and tape them together on the back. Display them and evaluate them individually or as a class.
7. As a further development of the design, trace it again on a piece of drawing paper and use colored pencils or colored markers to add color. Limit your colors and repeat them in a regular pattern so that they create a decorative design.

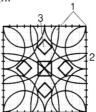

Assessments
- Guide the class in evaluating their individual tile designs.
- Complete your own evaluation of student designs for variety, creativity, and use of decorative color.

Lesson two: Pattern from a shape

Materials needed
- Bristol board or lightweight poster board
- pencils
- rulers
- compasses
- scissors or utility knives
- white drawing paper
- erasers
- fine-point black pen
- brown wrapping paper (optional)
- white tempera or white oil pastel (optional)
- colored pencils, crayons, or fine-point colored markers

Objectives

The students will do the following:

- Create an infinite repeat design by using overlapping shapes
- Use color to add to the decorative quality of the design

Procedure (pp. 38-39)

1. Choose a geometric shape and draw it on Bristol board as accurately as possible using a ruler, a compass, and geometric construction to aid you. Cut out your shape with scissors or a knife. This shape will be a pattern for your design.

2. Lay it on the drawing paper and trace around it. Move it to a position where it overlaps part of the first shape and trace it again. Look for interesting new shapes that are made by the crossing of the two original ones.

3. When you have found a pleasing combination, take a new piece of paper and begin tracing your shape, overlapping it to form the shape you liked. Be very consistent in how you overlap the shape each time. You may need to measure to keep the intervals regular in size. Fill the entire paper with the pattern. Do the tracing in pencil.

4. Now hang the design on the wall and look at it from a distance. If it looks too busy and the shapes are hard to see, try erasing one or more lines from the composition. Be sure to erase that same line or lines from all repetitions of the pattern.

5. When you are satisfied with the linear design, you can begin to fill in some of the spaces to make them solid or texture them with dots or lines. Use a variety of patterns so that the design will appear to have several different values when viewed from a distance. All this work should be done in black marker on white paper.

6. For a variation, try brown wrapping paper. Areas can be filled in with white tempera or textured with white oil pastel; others can be designed with black marker.

7. The same design can also be retraced and colored with colored pencil, crayons, or markers. Again, colors should be limited to a few and repeated regularly.

Assessments

- Guide the students in evaluating their work as they progress.
- Do your own evaluation of the large copies for variety of shapes, clarity, and decorative color.

Lesson three: Textile design

Materials needed

- design from previous project
- copier
- scissors
- one linoleum printing block for each student
- soft pencils, 2B or 3B or 1
- white paper
- masking tape
- #2 pencils
- fine-point permanent marker
- linoleum-cutting tools
- all-cotton fabric, washed and ironed and cut into one-yard squares
- plastic drop cloth
- textile printing ink in several colors
- scraps of sheet acrylic
- printing brayers (rollers)

Objective

The students will do the following:

- Choose a portion of one of their designs and print it on fabric

Procedure (pp. 39-40)

1. Choose one of your designs to use, preferably the black-and-white one. Copy it and reduce or enlarge it to a size appropriate for a textile design. Cut the design to a size that will fit on the linoleum block. Make sure that the design will interlock at the edges so that it can be repeated to make a continuous design.

2. With a soft pencil, redraw your design on white paper. Press hard so the pencil makes a dark line.

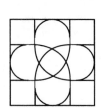

3. Turn the drawing pencil-side down on the linoleum block and tape it in place. Trace over the back of all the lines with a #2 pencil, pressing down to transfer the lines to the linoleum.

4. Remove the paper and tape. Check to make sure that all lines have been transferred. Trace over all lines with a fine-point permanent marker to keep them from smearing.

5. Use linoleum-cutting tools to cut away all the areas that will not print on the fabric. All lines and filled areas will remain raised; you will put ink on them to print. Carved-away areas will allow the fabric to show.

6. Choose a yard of all-cotton fabric of any color. It should be washed in hot water and detergent to remove the sizing added to it by the textile mill. Iron it smooth. (You can do this part of the project at home.)

7. Tape your fabric to a table covered with a plastic drop cloth.

8. Choose your ink color. Squeeze out about one inch from the tube onto a piece of sheet acrylic. Roll it out with the brayer until it is a uniform thickness. Then roll it onto the surface of the linoleum.

9. Turn your linoleum ink-side down and press it against the fabric. Apply pressure to the back. When you lift it, you will see your design transferred to the fabric. Do not be concerned if the ink does not always print solidly; a little texture usually helps the design.

10. Continue to ink and print your design until you have filled the fabric.

11. Read the directions on your textile ink to see what procedures you need to follow to set the color permanently.

12. To display these, tack them to a bulletin board and drape them.

Assessments

- Guide the students in evaluating their designs for color and size appropriate for textile application.
- Complete your own evaluation of the finished product for effective use of pattern and color for textile use.

Chapter 4: *Art on the Brink: Icons*

Seeing and Perceiving (pp. 45-47)

Questions and Answers

St. Nicholas the Wonderworker

1. Does the portrait have a realistic appearance? List several traits that make it unrealistic. *(The flat outlined shapes, the absence of blending and background, the patterns for hair and beard, and the people floating in little circles in the background tend to make the portrait less "real.")*

2. Can you point out the use of a pair of complementary colors? Icon painters liked intense color and particularly liked complementary colors for their contrast. *(The pairs of complementary colors are blue-green and red-orange.)*

3. Why do you think the painter used patterns of straight green lines in different values? *(He used these patterns to suggest the folds of the cloth in the garment.)*

4. The faces of icons are often recognizable. All icons of St. Nicholas portray him with a large forehead, receding hairline, and neatly curled beard. Let's examine the facial features of St. Nicholas. Which ones look as though the real features have been simplified according to a common style? *(The long, thin nose, the rounded eyebrows and shadows under the eyes, the almond-shaped eyes, the exaggerated cheekbones, and the patterns in the hair all reflect the common style. The folds in the garment also reflect this style.)*

Understanding and Evaluating (pp. 47-48)

Questions and Answers

1. What are some of the purposes for which people create paintings? *(They create paintings to show how things look, to share memories, to build civic pride, to glorify rulers, to express values, to tell stories, etc.)*

2. Are there several ways art can be used in religion? *(Art or craft objects can express beliefs, tell Bible stories, build up believers in the Faith, help create a worshipful atmosphere, aid in Christian services [as communion sets and offering plates do, for example], or receive worship. Although Christians would not approve of this last way, most would agree that the others are legitimate. At some time during the history of the church, art and craft objects have served all of these functions.)*

3. Look at the picture of St. Nicholas. What traits about the painting create a spiritual rather than earthly quality? *(The flatness, lack of background, lack of facial expression, lack of interaction with other people in the painting, and lack of motion all create a spiritual rather than earthly quality.)*

4. Can you see who is represented in the two circles at the top? *(Christ is on the left, and Mary is on the right.)*

5. Notice the object Nicholas is holding in his left hand. What is it? *(Nicholas is holding a gospel book with latches on the side and top, which kept the book closed.)*

6. Why do you think the book is drawn without perspective? *(It is drawn that way to maintain the overall flatness of the painting.)*

7. With the right hand, he is making a gesture. Traditionally this hand position was used for blessing. Is there any significance in the fact that he is blessing with the right hand? *(See Matthew 25:34.)*

Creative Expression Lessons

Lesson one: Study of medieval facial proportions

Materials needed
- compasses
- rulers
- pencils
- newsprint

Objective
The students will do the following:
- Use a typical medieval convention to organize a likeness of a person's face

Procedure (p. 49)

1. With a compass, draw three concentric circles so that the radius of the middle circle is twice that of the smallest and the radius of the largest is three times that of the smallest.

2. Following the Byzantine convention, sketch the features of a face on the three circles. Starting in the center circle, draw the nose from the middle to the bottom of the circle. Draw the height of the forehead on the top of the center circle. Place the eyes to each side of the bridge of the nose in the center of the circle. Draw the eyebrows a little above the eyes.

3. On the middle circle draw the chin at the bottom and draw the top of the head at the top. Fill the space between the forehead and top of the head with patterns that represent hair. Between the nose and chin draw the mouth.

4. Draw the neck down to the bottom of the largest circle and use the top of the circle to form the halo. The sides of the face do not fill up the circle; make the face oval.

5. Add shoulders and clothing.

Assessment
- Check the students' finished sketches for conventional proportion and added details.

Lesson two: Drawing an icon-style portrait
Materials needed
- white drawing paper
- compasses
- rulers
- pencils
- mirror (optional)

Objectives
The students will do the following:
- Review the conventional proportions of Byzantine icons
- Draw a portrait using the conventional proportions
- Combine individualized features with conventional proportions to make an icon-style portrait

Procedure (pp. 49-50)
1. Draw the three concentric circles very lightly on a piece of drawing paper or place a set of dark circles underneath so that they show through the paper.
2. Sketch the basic conventionalized outlines of a face.
3. Pair off with another student and draw each other or use a mirror to draw yourself.
4. Note the features of the face that make that individual or you look unique and sketch those features on the conventionalized sketch. Do not depart too far from the Byzantine model. Differences of hair, eyes, coloring, jewelry, and clothing will help your portrait look individual.

Assessments
- Hang the sketches up before class and have the students try to identify each person.
- Evaluate the portraits for both conventional representation and individual differences that identify the individual.

Lesson three: Painting an icon-style portrait
Materials needed
- Bristol board or poster board (7" × 12")
- tempera paints or acrylic paints
- assorted sizes of brushes
- Styrofoam plates for palettes

Objective
The students will do the following:
- Paint the portrait they drew using flat, intense colors. They may shade by using flat, unblended colors in three values, and they may add names or other objects that will help identify the person.

Procedure (p. 50)
1. Using the sketch you made in Lesson two, transfer your pencil sketch to a heavier paper.
2. Using tempera or acrylic, paint the background off-white or invent an architectural or landscape background appropriate for the portrait.
3. Paint the portrait in flat colors, starting with the darker ones and adding lighter tones. Folds of cloth can be painted with straight lines of various values. Do not be afraid to use intense and complementary colors. Colors will look better if they are mixed rather than used straight from the jar.
4. Icon painters sometimes lettered names on the background or included attributes so that viewers could identify the person in the picture. You may want to letter a name in the background or include some object that you associate with the person.

Assessments
- Guide the students in evaluating each other's paintings for their effectiveness in capturing the individual's personality.
- Evaluate the finished paintings, noting especially the use of medieval proportion, effective color combinations, and identifiable visual attributes.

Lesson four: Crayon batik
Materials needed
- washed, unbleached muslin
- pencils
- pieces of corrugated cardboard, a little larger than the muslin, with a square hole a little smaller than the muslin cut out of the center of each (or use wooden frames)
- masking tape
- permanent black marker pen
- thumbtacks, map pins, or sewing pins
- small pieces of old crayons, with paper removed
- small jars
- old electric skillet or shallow pan and electric hot plate
- old bristle brushes or cotton swabs
- large plastic bucket

- black fabric dye
- unprinted newsprint
- old electric iron
- needles and thread
- dowels
- embroidery floss and small glass beads (optional)

Objectives

The students will do the following:

- Use melted crayons and dye for color
- Create an icon-style portrait
- Add additional decoration with embroidery floss and/or small beads
- Plan and make a method of hanging the batik for display

Procedure (pp. 50-51)

1. Using one of your sketches from Lessons one or two, transfer it to washed, unbleached muslin with pencil.

2. Tape the muslin on cardboard and go over all lines with a permanent black marker pen.

3. Stretch the muslin on a wooden frame or cardboard with a square cut out of the center. Tack it around all the edges.

Use small map pins or sewing pins.

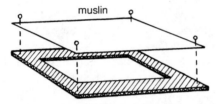

muslin

corrugated cardboard frame

4. Melt peeled crayons in small jars sitting in an inch of water in an electric skillet. Heat the water on medium heat until just boiling and adjust the temperature control so that it continues to boil gently until the crayons are melted. If the water boils dry, add more immediately. Your teacher will explain proper safety procedures when working with wax. See the list at the end of this section.

5. Using old bristle brushes or cotton swabs, paint the melted wax onto the cloth. Remember that the first color is the only one that will show, so do not overlap colors. Do not cover the black marker lines.

6. When the crayon wax is completely dry, dip the waxed cloth in black dye. Let it soak for several minutes. The longer it soaks, the darker the black will be. If you wish, you may wrinkle the waxed cloth before putting it in the dye. Be careful not to let wax chip off.

7. When the dye is completely dry, place the cloth between several layers of newsprint paper and iron it with a warm iron. As the paper absorbs wax, throw it away and add clean papers. Do not use newspapers because the ink may come off on your batik. When

you have ironed most of the wax out, the cloth will still be stiff.

8. Hem the edges or make fringes and hang the batik from a dowel stick.

9. You may add extra details with fine embroidery floss and small glass beads.

Safety procedures:

1. Keep wax in water when melting it. Unlike water, the temperature of wax continues to rise until it bursts into flame.

2. Keep a tight-fitting lid and/or fire extinguisher handy. Once burning, wax can be extinguished only by smothering it to cut off oxygen.

3. When wax is heated to a high temperature, it gives off a smoke that contains hazardous fumes. Keep the temperature low.

4. If wax gets on skin, it sticks and continues to burn. Keep a tub of ice water nearby so that the skin can be dipped in cold water to harden the wax and stop the burning.

Assessments

- Evaluate students' work habits and safety awareness.
- Evaluate their finished work for their use of medieval proportion and effective color combinations.

Chapter 5: International Gothic: Altarpieces

The Historical Background (p. 57)

Question and Answer

What is one of the first things you notice about it that identifies it as a Gothic painting? *(probably how the frame looks—it looks like a cathedral façade)*

Seeing and Perceiving (p. 58)

Questions and Answers

Virgin and Child with Saints

1. When did Niccolò paint this altarpiece? *(c. 1390)*
2. What does the date tell us about his painting style? *(It comes after the climax of Gothic; it shows the blending of northern and southern influences in his work.)*
3. At first glance, did you think the paintings looked realistic? *(probably not)*
4. Why or why not? *(Answers will vary.)*
5. Do the figures look at least a little rounded? *(yes)*
6. How did the artist make them look rounded? *(shading)*
7. Does there appear to be enough space behind them to walk between them and the background? *(Not really; it looks almost as if a wall is right behind them.)*
8. What is each of the figures doing? *(Nothing; each is simply standing still, looking toward the center, and holding something in his hands.)*
9. The painting is actually made up of a number of separate paintings. How many individual paintings do you see? *(There are eleven: five large panels, one in the predella, and five small circular paintings at the top.)*
10. Think back to what you learned about the techniques the artist used. Why would he make so many separate pieces? *(He was limited by the size of a wooden panel.)*
11. Why do you suppose the framer made so many deliberate references to a Gothic cathedral? *(He did so because the painting was made to go in a Gothic cathedral, so it imitates the style.)*
12. Suppose you were the painter and you were asked to do a large polyptych with a complex frame. What steps would you take, and in what order would you do them, to fulfill your commission? *(plan whom you wanted to include; research their lives; decide how large the panels would be; plan how many pieces you would need for the frame; prepare panels; gold leaf and paint panels; measure and cut frame pieces; glue them together; gold leaf the frame; mount the panels in it)*

Understanding and Evaluating (pp. 59-60)

Questions and Answers

1. How did Niccolò show John's attitude toward Christ in this picture? *(He points toward Jesus.)*
2. Now that you know the traditional story, you can also explain the other symbol found in the large panel of Mary. What does the small figure beside her represent? *(The figure represents a little angel feeding her.)*
3. The small figure seems to be holding a cup and a wafer. What is the significance of these two objects? *(A wafer and a chalice of wine represent the mass.)*
4. What aspects of the tradition about Mary's life sound to you as though they could really have happened? *(Going across the sea, seeing some Gauls converted, and living in the wilderness all seem plausible.)*
5. Which parts seem to be fictional? *(Going in a rudderless boat, converting all the Gauls, and being borne up and fed by angels definitely seem fictional.)*
6. Could some of these fictional elements be exaggerated versions of true events? *(Yes; some Gauls could have been saved; a church could have been established.)*
7. Could they be misunderstandings of figurative language? *(yes)*
8. Are these things also true of Mary? *(Yes; she sacrificed reputation and suffered sorrow.)*
9. Are they true of Jesus Christ Himself? *(Yes; He sacrificed heaven and His life on earth for us; He died almost alone, abandoned by all but a few followers.)*

Creative Expression Lessons

Lesson: Making a low-relief frame

Materials needed
- sample of your artwork
- sheets of white foam board
- rulers
- pencils
- mat knives or utility knives
- assorted objects (See Procedure #3 for suggestions.)
- acrylic gesso
- inexpensive craft brushes
- glue
- brown acrylic paint
- paper towels

Objective

The students will do the following:

- Plan and assemble various objects to create a richly decorative frame for one of their artworks

Procedure (pp. 60-61)

1. Choose a fairly small painting, drawing, print, or photograph that you have done.

2. You will have half a sheet of white foam board to use. Measure and draw the size and shape of your artwork in the center of the foam board. Measure a size one-eighth inch smaller on all sides and cut out the opening with a sharp mat knife.

3. Collect and bring to class an assortment of objects such as small dowels, twigs, pieces of wire, buttons, beads, paper clips, pull-tabs, snaps, old pencils or paint brushes, scraps of fabric trims, spiral macaroni, and so on. Place all the objects in one place to be available to the entire class.

4. Build up several of the areas of the frame with strips of foam board so that the frame begins to have a low relief structure. Choose several objects and arrange them on the foam board. Use enough of them to form a pattern. Repeat the pattern on each side of the frame to make a symmetrical design. Layer them on top of one another. Objects should not be easily identified when you are finished. The bottom of the frame should have more visual weight than the other sides so that it will look stable; the bottom can be thicker than the other sides. Edges of the foam board can be trimmed into shapes to fit the designs on the top. When you have decided which pieces you want to use, brush acrylic gesso on the foam board and on the pieces and glue them down. Start with the larger

objects first and glue the smaller ones on top of them. When all the objects have been adhered, paint acrylic gesso thinly over them. Do not cover up the textures of the objects. When you have finished, the entire frame should be nearly white. Strong colors may show through the gesso, but all the pieces should be covered.

5. Mix a stain of brown acrylic paint thinned with medium or water. Paint the stain over a part of the frame, letting it sink into the low areas. Blot it off the raised areas, creating an antiqued effect. If the foam board begins to curl, turn it over and paint gesso on the back.

Assessments

- Guide the students through an assessment of their individual work.
- Evaluate students' works based on how well they have achieved a symmetrical design with a variety of patterns, repetition of patterns, more visual weight at the bottom, and good craftsmanship in gluing and cutting.

Chapter 6: Portraits: the Art of Personality

Seeing and Perceiving (pp. 69-70)

Questions and Answers

1. Which one(s) is/are the most abstract? *(Eadwine the Scribe)* Which one(s) is/are the most realistic? *(Bindo Altoviti, Portrait of a Merchant, Edward VI as a Child, or Head of Christ. Students will have various opinions. Let them explain their choices.)*

2. What did the artist do that makes the portrait abstract or realistic looking? *(The flat shapes and outlines make it look abstract; three-quarter views and modeling in light and shade make it look more realistic.)*

3. Which ones look as though they are idealized? *(A Young Man in a Scarlet Turban, Ginevra dé Benci, and maybe Bindo Altoviti)* In what way do you think the person looked different from the way he or she is portrayed in the portrait? *(Student answers will vary, but following are some key ideas: A Young Man in a Scarlet Turban looks too stiff and seems to lack detail in the face; Ginevra would have had more bone structure and texture. Her hair would not have been quite so perfect, and she might have had more expression on her face. Bindo might have been a little less perfect than he looks here.)*

4. Which one(s) show(s) the deepest space behind the subject? *(Bindo Altoviti, Portrait of a Merchant)*

5. Which picture looks the flattest overall, including both subject and background? *(Eadwine the Scribe)*

6. Which one(s) contain(s) objects that show us something about the person's profession? *(Eadwine the Scribe, Portrait of a Merchant, Edward VI as a Child)* What is shown and what does it reveal about that profession? *(In Eadwine the Scribe there is a pen, a writing desk, and a cathedral in the background, showing that he works for the church and that his profession is that of a scribe. In Portrait of a Merchant there are papers in the background to show his system of keeping records and how busy and important he is. Edward VI holds a scepter that symbolizes his future royal rule.)*

7. In each picture, what do the clothes tell us about the person? *(Eadwine's tell us that he is a monk; the young man in the turban wears fancy clothes and an elaborate head covering that show his wealth and taste for the exotic; Ginevra and Bindo wear the current styles of clothing that indicate wealth and social position. The merchant is apparently wearing his normal dress for work. Edward VI's clothes show his royal status as the only son of the king. In the Head of Christ the clothes are very generic; they do not*

show anything, or perhaps they are the common clothes of a worker.)*

Understanding and Evaluating (pp. 70-73)

Questions and Answers

Eadwine the Scribe

1. In Eadwine's self-portrait, we see a medieval man displaying pride not only in what he is doing but also in who he is. Look at the edges and background of the portrait. How do we know when he lived? *(The architecture looks Gothic; his chair and the base of his desk have Gothic designs too.)*

2. The portrait is painted in a pose traditionally used to show philosophers. The Christians had always used this pose to show the inspired writers of the Bible. Why do you think Eadwine used this pose for his portrait? *(He is elevating himself and his profession to be equal with philosophers and apostles by using this pose.)*

3. Around the outside of the portrait, in the form of a riddle, the monk wrote, "Neither my fame nor my praise will die quickly; demand of my letters who I am. . . . Fame proclaims you in your writing for ever Eadwine, you are to be seen here in the painting. The worthiness of this book demonstrates your excellence. O God, this book is given to You by him. Receive this acceptable gift." What is Eadwine so proud of? *(Eadwine is proud of his letters or calligraphy in the book.)*

4. Donald Jackson, the official scribe to the Queen of England, commented: "We hope God was grateful!" Why does he say that? *(Eadwine's statement seems to assume He ought to be; Eadwine seems conceited.)*

Ginevra dé Benci

5. What does this symbolic emblem add to your knowledge of the woman? *(Perhaps she had been victorious in some trial or exhibited high character or virtue. Perhaps she was known for her virtue.)*

6. This picture was highly praised by contemporaries for its lifelikeness. Does she look like a great beauty to you? How has taste in feminine beauty changed since this portrait was made? *(Answers will vary.)*

Bindo Altoviti

7. What is the young man doing? *(He is turning to look at us; students may have other speculations.)*

8. What kind of personality do you think he had? *(Answers will vary, but make sure students can give reasons for their opinions.)*

9. If you did not know that he was a wealthy business-man, what would you think he did for a living? *(Answers will vary.)*

10. How does Bindo Altoviti's portrait compare to Ginevra's? *(His portrait looks more three-dimensional, not as flat as Ginevra's; it is more realistic.)*

Portrait of a Merchant

11. Let's compare Jan Gossaert's *Portrait of a Merchant* with Raphael's *Bindo Altoviti*. What is similar about the two portraits? What is different? (Similar: *They are both wealthy businessmen. They both look very serious. They are both shown indoors. Both artists paint solid, three-dimensional figures.* Different: *Bindo is shown without any objects to identify him. We have to be told that he is a patron of the arts. The merchant is at work with his papers all around him. Bindo seems to be dressed more lightly than the merchant. This would be due to the warmer climate in Italy. The painting of Bindo seems more unified than that of the merchant.)*

12. The details he included in the environment of the merchant help Gossaert show us the ordinary activities of his profession. Imagine that you are actually there. What was this man doing just before you walked in? *(It looks as if we interrupted him in his work.)*

13. Is he happy to see you? *(Not very; he looks as though he would prefer we hurry with our business.)*

14. What are all the papers on the back wall? *(Perhaps they are papers from customers.)*

15. Does the painting have a clear center of interest? If so, what is it? If not, why not? *(No. It seems to divide our attention between his face, the papers on the wall, and the paper on his desk; they are all about equally important.)*

Edward VI as a Child

16. If you did not know he was a prince, how could you tell from the portrait? *(He wears lavish clothes and holds a golden object in his hand.)*

17. Does he look like a normal two year old? If not, what is different? *(He gives a royal gesture of greeting. He is a child, yet he seems already a king.)*

Head of Christ

18. How many different values can you see in the shadows? *(three or four)*

19. Look at the line between the hair and face. Why is it so blended? *(It is blended to keep it from looking cut out; the blending makes it look more realistic.)*

20. Rembrandt painted much more freely than many of his contemporaries. Can you see brush strokes of unblended paint? *(yes, in the background, hair, robe, and beard)*

21. A very important characteristic of Rembrandt's painting is his ability to make the form look three-dimensional. Compare *Head of Christ* with *Ginevra*

dé Benci. (Leonardo's portrait looks like an inflated balloon—it has little bone structure underlying the skin. Rembrandt's Head of Christ *is more lifelike. The artist's subtle use of highlights and shadows creates a more defined human form.)*

22. There is another comparison we can make. Christ looks out directly to us as though He will speak. Which other portraits seem to reveal a personality, not just an outward likeness? *(Raphael's; Gossaert's does a little, but not with a kindly expression; Holbein's)*

Match the following statements with the portraits: This artist is most interested in

23. putting us directly in the presence of the person. *(Raphael, Holbein, Gossaert, Rembrandt)*

24. impressing us with the social rank of the person. *(Holbein)*

25. showing us the noble features of the person. *(Masaccio, Raphael)*

26. exalting the character qualities of the person. *(Leonardo, Holbein)*

27. elevating his own rank and workmanship. *(Eadwine)*

28. showing us the profession of the person. *(Eadwine, Gossaert)*

29. showing us the personality of the person. *(Rembrandt, Raphael, Gossaert)*

Creative Expression Lessons

Lesson one: Pattern portrait

Materials needed
- white drawing paper, 9" × 12"
- pencils
- erasers
- black waterproof fine-point marker
- colored pencils, watercolor, or water-based markers

Objectives
The students will do the following:
- Draw a likeness of a friend's face
- Fill the clothing area with flat patterns
- Fill the background with drawings of objects that relate to the student's surroundings, life, or interests

Procedure (p. 75)
1. Pair off with another student. By facing each other, you can draw each other simultaneously.
2. Make a line drawing of the face with no shading or any attempt to make the portrait three-dimensional looking.
3. Draw in the general outlines of the body and clothing of the person.
4. Patterns used for the clothing may be based upon those on the actual clothing or you can make them up. Avoid patterns that are too intricate because they will take too long and be indistinguishable.

5. Include in the background objects seen in the room, such as chairs or tables, or objects that show some facet of the sitter's interests, such as sporting equipment, books, bicycles, and so forth. Draw these objects as flat as the designs in the clothing.

6. Once all the parts of the portrait are drawn, go over the lines with a black waterproof marker. Lines may vary in thickness, but they will show in the final artwork.

7. Color objects, designs, and the person, using colored pencils, watercolor, or colored water-based markers. Limit your colors to five or six and repeat these colors for a decorative color scheme.

Assessment
- Look for flat patterns, repeated colors, and background objects that identify the subject of the portrait.

Lesson two: Profile portraits
Materials needed
- newsprint for short practices
- pencils
- white drawing paper for the longer drawing
- interesting hats for the longer drawing

Objective
The students will do the following:
- Draw profiles of several other students in class, including hairstyles or hats and clothing

Procedure (p. 75)
1. You will alternate between modeling for others and drawing in a series of ten- or fifteen-minute drawings.

2. Draw at least four profile drawings of four different people in class. Draw in line only, and do not hurry. Make the lines light but definite, not sketchy, especially as the exercise continues and you gain confidence.

3. After you have gained confidence and the drawings are improving in accuracy and proportion, do two longer sessions. Pair off and spend half the class period drawing each other's profiles.

4. You may shade this drawing, and you may include more details of clothing and hair or hats. Bring interesting hats to class for the longer portrait.

Assessments
- Guide the students in evaluating their own short poses. (The class may evaluate the longer pose.)
- Evaluate the long pose for its resemblance to the model and interesting details of hair, hat, jewelry, garment, and so forth.

Lesson three: Three-quarter-view portrait
Materials needed
- chair
- floodlights with clamps to position them
- plain, dark background
- white drawing paper, 12" × 18"
- soft drawing pencils, 2B-3B
- erasers
- drawing boards a little larger than the paper
- colored pencils or oil pastels

Objective
The students will do the following:
- Draw a lifelike three-quarter-view portrait and color it with colored pencils

Procedure (p. 76)
1. Your teacher will bring someone from outside the class to model for class members during the portrait lesson. The drawing will be a portrait bust and will include a plain background. The model will wear the same clothing for each modeling session. Seat the model comfortably against a plain, preferably dark background. Floodlights should be shining from above and to one side.

2. You will choose a point of view from which to draw the model, paying close attention to your position so that you will be able to duplicate it in each drawing session.

3. Use good quality drawing paper for this project so it can withstand reworking. Make the initial drawing very light, just placing the drawing of the model on the page and indicating proportions. Draw the portrait in pencil with light lines; do as little erasing as possible.

4. When the drawing is complete, color the portrait (including the background) with colored pencils or oil pastels. Blend the colors to achieve a wide variety of colors and a range of values.

Assessments
- Have the class vote for the most successful portraits.
- Evaluate them on solidity of facial structure, use of color value to model the form, and inclusion of interesting details.

Chapter 7: Michelangelo, Painter of the Sistine Ceiling

Seeing and Perceiving (p. 82)

Questions and Answers

The Prophet Joel and *Libyan Sibyl*

1. What similarities do you notice? (*Both are sitting on a throne, both look as though they are thinking about what they have read, both are wearing colorful robes, both are barefoot, and both have little figures beside them.*)

2. What differences do you notice? (*One is a man, one a woman; the sibyl's robes are more colorful; Joel has a scroll—the sibyl has a book; the sibyl looks larger—she seems to fill the space more.*)

3. Which of the two figures looks more massive and three-dimensional? (*The Libyan sibyl looks much taller and bigger than the prophet Joel.*)

4. Look specifically at the footrest at the bottom of the throne. How did Michelangelo find room to make the sibyl larger? (*He moved the footrest down farther between the windows and made it narrower.*)

5. Why do you think Michelangelo made the later figures bigger than the early ones? (*Maybe he felt they could not be seen well enough from below; maybe he felt they were important enough to be made larger than any of the other figures.*)

6. See if you can point out some of these changes in the two figures. (*Joel's right hand and foot create a line almost exactly parallel to the painted molding over the window. His other leg forms a diagonal that repeats the molding on the other side. The sibyl's upper body is parallel to the molding on the left and a line drawn from her hip to her right foot parallels the molding on the right. [See diagram 7-4 on page 81 of the student text]. Michelangelo surrounds the sibyl with more robes and allows them to spill over on each side so that they cover the entire seat and arms of the throne. Joel's robes stay much closer to him, and more of the seat can be seen. The sibyl's costume has much more color and decoration than Joel's grayish one. The size of the sibyl and the shading create a feeling of a massive figure more than the figure of Joel does. Her pose is certainly more twisted than his.*)

Understanding and Evaluating (pp. 82-85)

Questions and Answers

1. According to this standard, how effective are these paintings? (*They are very effective; they look like painted sculpture.*)

2. Which one seems more contemplative? (*Joel seems more contemplative. He seems to be just sitting, reading his scroll. He seems to look a little surprised as though he has read something he did not expect to find. In I Peter 1:10-11, Peter indicates that prophets did not always understand what they were writing.*)

3. Which seems more active? (*The Libyan sibyl looks as if she has just laid down her book and is about to step down and do something.*)

4. What do the little genii figures tell you about Joel? (*One of Joel's genii seems to be ordering the other one to do something; he has his book closed, and it is time for action.*)

5. List the events referred to in the poem. (*The events are the Crucifixion, the darkening of the sun, the earthquake, and the resurrection of the dead.*)

6. How many expressions can you find in which Michelangelo expressed a visual idea? (*Such expressions include "opened heaven's doors," "blood-dripping sepulcher," "man's ancient blur," "became a slave to slaves," "stars darkened," "mountains quaked," "seas were tossed and torn," "dark abode," and "ugly angels sank in fiercer woe."*)

7. Who is the person referred to as "you" in the first four lines? (*The person is Christ.*)

8. Who are the "blessed spirits"? (*They are the angels.*)

9. Why are the blessed spirits both glad and sad to see the Crucifixion? (*They are glad because of man's redemption and because they did not have to suffer; they are sad because of the suffering Christ had to bear to provide man's redemption.*)

10. Who are the "ugly angels" in line 13? (*They are demons or fallen angels.*)

11. Knowing what you have read about Neo-Platonism, why did Michelangelo call them ugly? (*Since he believed that beauty comes from God, all that is God-cursed must be ugly.*)

Creative Expression Lessons

Lesson one: Detail study

Materials needed
- white or manila paper, 9" × 12"
- soft drawing pencils, 2B or 3B
- masking tape (optional)

Objective
The students will do the following:
- Draw and shade sketches of hands, feet, face, etc. (Begin by using the blind contour method.)

Procedure (pp. 85-86)

1. Pair off with another student.

2. Using 9" × 12" paper and soft drawing pencils, do blind contours of each other. Concentrate on one part at a time: the head, a profile perhaps, or a hand or arm, even a foot.

3. In the blind contour method, the artist looks only at the model, not at the paper, guiding his pencil by moving it at the same speed and in the same direction as his eye moves along the contour. You may look down from time to time to maintain the proportion. You may also draw your own hand by taping down the paper and posing your nondrawing hand.

4. Draw several sketches of heads, hands, arms, or feet. As you draw, try to look more at the model than the paper.

Assessment

• Observe the students while they draw. Blind contour does not usually produce "finished" works. Drawing will often be inconsistent in proportion, and parts may not line up. The method's main purpose is to train the eye and hand to work together, so do not grade contour drawings on proportion or finished quality.

Lesson two: Unity through grouping

Materials needed

• old magazines
• scissors
• double-sided transparent tape
• white drawing paper, 18" × 12"
• glue sticks or other paper paste
• colored pencils or watercolors and brushes

Objectives

The students will do the following:

• Cut out several figures from old magazines
• Arrange them into two or three groupings and paste them down

Procedure (p. 86)

1. Search through old magazines for pictures of figures to cut out. A variety of sizes may be used.

2. Tack the figures down temporarily to a piece of paper using double-sided tape.

3. Hang the papers up in front of the class and notice the lack of unity, especially when viewed from the back of the room.

4. Now rearrange the figures in groups. You may use overlapping, proximity, or something in the background to unify the groups. Paste them down.

5. Display the completed compositions before the class and compare them to the original paste-up in step two.

6. As a further development of this idea, cut out more figures and think of an action that will help unify the group. Illustrate a background for the activity. You may combine your illustration with magazine collage. Remember to use background elements to unify the figures.

7. Paste the cut-out figures over the illustrated background.

Assessments

• Have the class evaluate the first non-unified composition.

• Evaluate the group composition and/or the illustrated one.

Lesson three: Fresco painting

Materials needed

• fiberboard, finished on one side and cut into small panels for each student
• manila paper the same size as the fiberboard panels
• pencils
• watercolor paints
• brushes
• 5 lb. container of ready-to-use spackling paste
• trowel or wide spackling knife
• backboard molding (optional)

Note: All these materials can be purchased at a building supply store.

Objectives

The students will do the following:

• Draw a face or a still life
• Paint it in fresco

Procedure (pp. 86-87)

1. Draw a simple subject (such as a face) or a single object. Keep the subject large and simple. It should almost fill the paper. This is your cartoon.

2. Plan the colors on the cartoon with watercolor.

3. When the cartoon is ready, prepare the fresco panel: use a piece of fiberboard that is rough on the back side. The fiberboard should be the same size and proportion as the cartoon. Apply wet spackling paste to the fiberboard with a trowel or wide spackling knife. Let it dry long enough to be firm but not dry.

4. When the plaster is firm, transfer the cartoon to it. Lay your cartoon over the plaster and trace over the lines with a sharp pencil. Lines will show up as grooves in the plaster.

5. Paint on the damp surface with watercolor paints. Continue to work as long as the spackling paste remains damp. Start out with very light colors and darken them gradually by adding darker layers. Avoid mixing too many colors together and thereby making muddy colors. Colors that are too dark or muddy cannot be removed. Avoid using too much water or too much brushing—it may soften the spackling paste too much.

6. Lay the painting flat to dry.

7. If desired, frame the panels with simple molding.

Assessment

- Have the students evaluate their own cartoon before you evaluate the finished work.

Note: Students may need to do several of these before they understand how to work with the medium.

Chapter 8: Landscapes of the Heart, Eye, and Mind

The Artists (p. 91)

Questions and Answers

The Blind Bartimaeus and *Self-Portrait*

1. Look at the picture of *The Blind Bartimaeus*. How does the painting affect you? *(Answers will vary.)* What specific things about the painting contribute to this effect? *(The dark background, uncertain lighting, posture and facial expression, clothes, and lack of background details all contribute to the effect.)*

2. Look at the detail from *Self-Portrait*. Do you think *The Blind Bartimaeus* may be a self-portrait? *(Answers will vary.)* If it is, does that change your outlook on Salvator Rosa as a person? *(Pessimism may be due to depression over his problems.)*

The Historical Background (pp. 93-94)

Questions and Answers

Eclogue IV and Isaiah 11:1-10

1. What aspects of nature are named in both quotations? *(goats, flocks, lion, serpent)*

2. Which aspects are named only in one? (Virgil: *flowers and poison plants;* Isaiah: *wolf, lamb, leopard, bear, calf, ox, cow*)

3. The most important difference between the two selections is the power that will accomplish the remaking of the earth. Virgil cannot name any power that is able to transform man and nature so dramatically. Read verses 1-3 of the Isaiah passage to find out what power will accomplish the task. *(The rod, the stem of Jesse, and the Branch are all symbols of Christ, upon whom the Spirit of the Lord rests.)*

Seeing and Perceiving (pp. 94-99)

Questions and Answers

Sacred Conversation

1. Look at Bonifazio's *Sacred Conversation*. Notice how the figures make a continuous screen across the foreground of the picture. They seem to close off any possible view into the distance except for one place at the right side. What do you see there? *(a road leading to a castle or town)*

2. How far is it from the figure at the right to the castle? *(a comfortable walking distance, on the edge of town)*

3. Do you see anything in the middle ground? *(There seems to be a tree, but we cannot see the ground.)*

4. Notice the colors used by Bonifazio for the landscape section of his picture. How do they help create the convincing effect of distance? *(The mountains in the distance are blue and hazy.)*

5. What other devices does he use to create the illusion of distance? *(He uses less detail in the distance; distant objects are higher up in the picture; sizes are smaller in the distance; there is less contrast of value or color in the distance.)*

The Hiding of Moses

6. Sébastien Bourdon's *The Hiding of Moses* includes most of the typical features. Can you identify each of them? *(The painting has the following elements of the typical classical landscape: a dark tree at one side; a group of trees on the opposite side; a ground that extends across the front of the picture plane, defining the foreground of the picture; a group of small figures in the center; some classical-looking architecture nestled in hills and trees; a clear sky with mounds of cumulus clouds.)*

7. Examine the mountains. They are not the small mountains that Bonifazio painted. Review Sébastien's travels. Where could he have seen mountains like these? *(the Alps in northern Italy)*

8. What is the story being told? *(See Exodus 2:1-3.)*

9. How do the parents feel about what they are doing? *(They are sad, especially Moses' father.)* How does the artist convey their feelings? *(He conveys their feelings by their posture.)*

10. What allusions does Bourdon make to ancient history, when this story took place? *(The sculpture and columns at the front, the classical architecture of the town, and the old-fashioned costumes all allude to ancient history.)*

11. Has he made his scene look like the actual country where this event happened? *(Not generally. Neither the architecture nor land looks Egyptian.)*

12. How did Bourdon solve the problem of a jump from foreground to background? *(He fills the space with water running diagonally back into the space and dividing to the right and left.)*

13. The composition has a calm, organized look in spite of the attempt to arouse pity for the grieving parents. Although not as obvious as the light filling the scene, the actual structure of the painting also helps to create this sense of calmness. The painting has many geometric shapes and forms. Name as many geometric shapes or forms as you can find in the painting. *(square, part of a circle, vertical cylinders, rectangles, triangles, arches, and a rectangle with a half circle on top)*

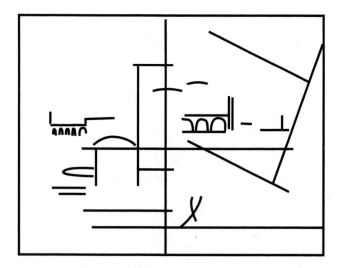
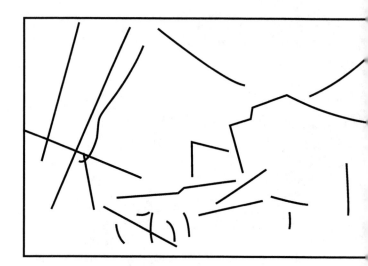

14. Using a piece of tracing paper, trace all the horizontal and vertical lines. Where do the most lines occur? *(left front, about one-third of the width of the painting)* Where are the strongest verticals in the painting? *(the two columns to the left of center and the figure of the father)* Where is the strongest horizontal? *(the top of the monument behind them)* Those two lines divide the painting into four nearly even rectangles.

15. There is one very prominent slanted line. What is it? *(tree at the right)*

16. Bourdon follows his teacher Poussin in the way he constructed his painting. Whenever Poussin included a slanted line, he found a way to include another line perpendicular to it. Can you find two lines perpendicular to the slanted line? *(The top edge of the bushes in the foreground makes a line perpendicular with the tree; the right slope of the mountains in the background does too.)*

17. There are at least four other examples of this perpendicular angle. Can you find them? *(heads of Moses' parents; three triangular gables in the background)*

Landscape with the Baptism of Christ

18. Examine the painting *Landscape with the Baptism of Christ*. What is happening in the little group at the edge of the water? *(baptism of Christ by John the Baptist)*

19. Does this event seem more or less important than the rest of the picture? Why? *(Student opinions may vary; however, the subject seems less important because of its small size.)*

20. How does he show the distance of the far valley? *(He uses a lighter color, less contrast, less detail, and fewer hard edges.)*

21. As you examine the painting, what impressions do you get of this place? *(Either of the following two views may be expressed: calm, warm, sunny, afternoon; or volcanic rocks, lightning-struck trees, storm clouds coming. In either case, encourage the students to explain their responses.)*

22. In contrast to Bourdon's ideal landscape, Salvator Rosa uses diagonal lines to organize his composition. Take a piece of tracing paper as you did before and trace all the diagonal lines. Do the two diagrams give you different feelings? *(The first one gives a square, man-made, organized feeling; the second one gives a feeling of things falling or moving. Students may have other ways of expressing these ideas. Listen for the ideas, not the specific wording.)*

23. Where is the center of interest? *(Students will have varying impressions; they should support their views with reasons; actually there is not a clear one.)*

24. How many details can you see that demonstrate natural power? *(The cliffs are volcanic forms; the trees growing out of cliffs, the lightning-split trees, and the storm clouds on the horizon all illustrate natural power.)*

25. What evidence of man's civilization do you see? *(There is a structure in the far valley.)*

Understanding and Evaluating (pp. 99-101)

Questions and Answers

Landscape with the Baptism of Christ

1. Do these people seem to be aware of the importance of what is going on? *(Student answers will vary.)*

2. Contrast their actions with those of today's spectators at an event with a notable celebrity. Does the picture illustrate truthfully the life and ministry of Christ? *(Possibly, since He was rejected and misunderstood by His contemporaries. They failed to understand who He was or why He came. It was not until they could get something tangible that they came in large crowds to see Him.)*

3. Do those broken, windswept trees and cliffs symbolize a truth about Christ? *(They could symbolize the hardships in His or the nation's past; they could symbolize violent past events.)*

4. What about the sky at the left side of the picture? What might it mean? *(It looks as though a fierce storm is coming; Jesus' future was not a sunny, calm life but was filled with storms.)*

5. It has been said that pictures cannot illustrate either a past or a future time. Is that true of this picture? *(no)*

6. Which parts seem to illustrate a past event? Which parts may illustrate the future? *(Trees and cliffs were formed in the past; baptism is the present; the storm seems to be threatening in the immediate future; the calm valley could be the promise of a more distant future.)*

The Hiding of Moses

7. Another classical idea demonstrated by Bourdon is his characterizations of the father and mother. Notice their postures. If you draw one line through each figure that represents the general position of the figure, what kind of line would describe the father's position? *(vertical)*

8. What kind of line describes the mother? *(curved)*

9. There are several small figures beyond the rock just above the monument. One seems to be a soldier in a Roman-looking helmet; the others are women holding infants. What do they add to the painting? *(They add background to the story; Egyptian officials were killing all baby boys. That was why Moses' parents hid him.)*

10. Compare Bourdon's painting to Salvator Rosa's. Which one makes better use of the sky to help convey the emotional atmosphere of the story? Why? *(Probably Salvator Rosa's; it adds to the story; Bourdon's does not convey the sadness of the event.)*

11. Does Bourdon include anything that might hint of the future of Moses? *(If you follow the branch of the river to the left, it seems to lead away from Egypt.)*

Sacred Conversation

Goldfinches	Christ's suffering because goldfinches are supposed to eat thorns
Butterfly	resurrection: caterpillar to pupa to butterfly
Baby rabbits	defenselessness; at Mary's feet they symbolize triumph over lust
Red	*love, sacrifice; Mary and Jesus*
Blue	heaven and truth; fidelity; also Mary and Jesus
Green	life, especially triumph of life over death
White	*innocence, purity, virginity*

Yellow	divinity, faith, fruitfulness, illumination of truth
Open books	*learning, Bible; wisdom and truth*
Palm branches	victory over death; martyrdom
Marble platform	separation of the sacred from the commonplace
Laurel wreaths	*victory; laurel is evergreen; Roman athletic prize*
Cross	*the Crucifixion foretold*
Leather garment	*John the Baptist, clothed with camel's skin*
Ferocious lion	"The devil, as a roaring lion, walketh about, seeking whom he may devour" (I Pet. 5:8).
Broken column	Christ's suffering; He was tied to a column and whipped
Green tree	*life*

12. In the other two paintings, the landscapes add meaning to the story. Does the landscape in Bonifazio's painting add to its meaning? Why or why not? *(Not really; it contains no symbols that relate to the story.)*

Creative Expression Lessons

Lesson one: Seeing the abstract underlying the real

Materials needed
- books or magazines or photocopies of Renaissance or baroque paintings
- tracing paper, 9" × 12"
- pencils and erasers
- white drawing paper
- colored pencils

Objectives
The students will do the following:
- Make a line analysis of a painting
- Use that analysis to create an abstract composition

Procedure (p. 101)
1. Choose a reproduction of a Renaissance or baroque painting. Lay a piece of tracing paper over the reproduction and trace major lines of the composition. Trace them only where they actually occur: do not extend them or connect two lines unless they connect in the painting. They may be vertical, horizontal, diagonal, or curved lines. Trace around the edge of the reproduction.

2. Lightly retrace all the lines onto white drawing paper with pencil. You may now extend one or two off the edges. You may eliminate some of the short lines. You should keep the same composition, but simplify some of the busy areas. Use colored pencils to place colored shapes in some of the spaces. Keep the same center of interest that the original artist had, but you may use other colors. Not all the spaces should have color in

them. You may make the shapes have soft instead of hard edges. By the sizes of shapes and colors used, you can re-create the same focal point.

Assessment

• Compare each student's tracing with a photocopy of the original painting to make sure it represents the composition of the picture. Check for similarity to the original composition and the same focal point. Sizes, shapes, and colors should lead the eye to the same point used by the original artist.

Lesson two: Composing a landscape

Materials needed

• old magazines with colored pictures (or other sources)
• scissors
• Bristol board
• old newspapers
• acrylic mat medium
• old paint brushes
• waxed paper, plastic bags, or plastic sheeting

Objective

The students will do the following:

• Cut out various parts of a landscape from magazine photos and assemble them to make a larger landscape

Procedure (pp. 101-2)

1. From some old magazines, travel brochures, or travel posters, you will choose various elements from different photographs: perhaps a dramatic sky from one, mountains from another, and buildings or close-up plants from another. Tear or cut out the entire photos. When you have decided which elements you want to use, trim them carefully along the edges of the shapes. You may even add clouds to a sky this way. If you cut carefully, the objects will look like part of the same picture.

2. Arrange your parts so that the nearer ones overlap the more distant. Work on composition: defining a focal point, using lines to lead the eye to the focal point, and including interesting details. Do not make the same mistake many Renaissance artists did; include some area of middle ground so that the scene recedes smoothly from front to back.

3. When you have all the pieces you need and have determined their arrangement, glue them down to a piece of Bristol board. Start with the sky; turn the picture over on a piece of newspaper and paint acrylic mat medium on the back of it. Lay it on the Bristol board and gently smooth out any wrinkles. Be sure it is well-adhered all over. Then glue on the next most distant object overlapping the sky. Continue gluing all the pieces from the farthest to the nearest. As you work, the Bristol board will begin to curl up. To correct this, lay it on a piece of waxed paper or plastic sheeting and paint the back with acrylic medium. It

may take several coats of medium on the back to correct the curl. Covering the picture with waxed paper and putting it under a heavy weight overnight will also help to correct the curling. Do not cover the picture with newspaper because the newspaper will stick in the medium and ruin the picture.

Note: Do not allow the medium to dry in the brushes.

Assessments

• Demonstrate the trimming and overlapping of two items to make them look as though they are one unit.
• Guide the students through a class evaluation of the best composition: lines leading the eye to the focal point, degree of interest in composition, and smooth transition from front to back.
• Evaluate all the students' landscapes.

Lesson three: Watercolor painting based on the landscape collage

Materials needed

• student-grade watercolor paper
• pencils and erasers
• black thread, tape, and rulers (optional)
• watercolors (tubes of assorted colors or pan watercolors)
• Styrofoam plates to use as palettes
• watercolor brushes in assorted sizes (Start out with large ones; use small ones only for finishing details.)
• water jars
• paper towels

Objectives

The students will do the following:

• Sketch the landscape from their photo collage onto a large piece of watercolor paper
• Paint the landscape in watercolor

Procedure (pp. 102-3)

1. Using very light pencil lines, sketch the landscape from your photo collage onto a piece of watercolor paper. Sketch by eye and keep the proportions the same as they were in the collage. You may find it helpful to divide the collage into four equal parts by wrapping black thread around the middle vertically and horizontally. Tape the thread in back so that it can be removed when you are finished. Lightly divide your watercolor paper into equal fourths also. Now you can copy the parts of the landscape easily onto the watercolor paper. Do not mechanically enlarge the collage.

2. Decide which parts of your painting will be white. In watercolor, white is made by letting the paper show through, so it is very important to plan ahead. Thin down the sky color and modify it with small amounts of other colors. The first colors you apply should be mostly water. Before painting, wet the entire sky area with water. Dot the sky color onto the wet paper. Add

some other colors for variety. Leave some areas white for clouds. If you want a stormy sky, add some slightly darker grays or reds. When the paint starts to dry, leave it alone. Color may be blotted out of the clouds with a tissue, but otherwise do not touch the painting.

3. When the sky is almost dry, you can add some pale blue or purple for distant mountains. Let the color run into the sky a little to give it a soft edge.

4. Once the entire sky is dry, mix the colors you will need for the middle ground. Remember to use mostly water. Avoid painting over areas where there will be objects in the foreground. Paint trees, fields, hills, and so forth with thin paint. Use various shades of green for variety. Add more water for lighter areas and more paint for darker areas. Remember that the paint should always be transparent. Don't be too fussy. Let the shapes be free and leave some white paper showing.

5. Foreground objects can be added with the same transparent paint. In the foreground use more variety of color and value. Always keep the color transparent.

6. When all the paint has dried, add blue washes to the shadows to cool them and add pale yellow washes to the sunlit areas.

7. Extra details may be added to the foreground. Painting with an almost dry brush will add texture to tree trunks, blades of grass, and other details. Some shapes can be outlined to make them clearer. Small branches and twigs on trees are drawn with the dry brush. Avoid getting too fussy with these details, though. The painting should stay loose and free and transparent. You are now learning that watercolor is not an easy medium. You will need lots of practice to learn to use it well.

Assessments
- Allow students to do two or three of these and choose the best one for grading.
- Evaluate the painting for transparency of watercolor, freedom of execution, and relationship of foreground, middle, and background.

Lesson four: On-site landscape drawing

Materials needed
- viewfinders (a 3" × 5" card with a rectangle cut out of the middle)
- drawing paper
- masking tape
- drawing boards at least as large as the paper (Fiberboard works well for drawing boards.)
- drawing pencils, 1B or 2B
- erasers
- newsprint scraps

Objective
The students will do the following:
- Choose a part of the scene that has a pleasing composition and sketch the major details of the scene

Procedure (p. 103)
1. Your class will take a field trip to a local scenic area with a variety of landscape views. Choose which view you want.

2. By positioning your hands or using viewfinders, determine whether you will need a horizontal or vertical format.

3. With the paper taped to a drawing board, sketch the major forms. Start out very lightly and loosely since dark lines are impossible to erase. Look for the relationships of one object to another. Eliminate or replace what is too hard to see or what you do not understand. When the sketch is complete, put another paper under your hand so that you will not smear your sketch as you begin to add more detail.

4. Place the most detail in the foreground objects. If you have enough time, you may begin to shade the picture. Begin in the focal point and work out from there. This drawing should take several visits to the site to complete. You may want to use this drawing to make a watercolor too.

Assessments
- Demonstrate how to use the hands as a viewfinder or how to use a paper viewfinder.
- Evaluate the drawing for composition, sense of space, detail in foreground, and format.

Chapter 9: Tintoretto, Spacial Expressions

Seeing and Perceiving (pp. 110-12)

Questions and Answers

The Visit of the Queen of Sheba to Solomon

1. Point out each of these devices in the picture. *(Many of the figures are leaning or turning so that their bodies form curved lines; there are two groups on the left and right who look as though they are conversing; the figure in the front with her back to us is the repoussoir figure; strong colors are used in the various clothes; and shimmering highlights can be seen in the queen's dress, the repoussoir figure, and the exotic garment at the left side.)*

2. Examine the small figures in the background detail. Why do you think Tintoretto painted them like that? *(He did so to make them look as though they were in the distance with less detail and perhaps because he was working fast.)*

3. Another Tintoretto technique was to place the entire foreground in open shade with a lighter area behind it to show space. Do you see where he cautiously put some shade in the foreground? *(At the left near the building there is a shade line showing on the pavement.)*

4. Critics have observed that Tintoretto is not always consistent about his light sources. Can you see any place where he has been inconsistent in this picture? *(There is a very dark shadow under the repoussoir figure, but shadows of other people and objects are not always as dark. Shadows lie in different directions on the ground. The shadow of the exotic figure at the left points back toward the queen, while the shadows of the vases point almost straight sideways.)*

5. What part of the scriptural story is taking place in this work? *(Answers will vary, but students should explain their opinions by what they see in the painting.)*

6. How does Tintoretto show that space in *The Visit of the Queen of Sheba to Solomon*? *(by making the checkered floor and spacing the figures out on it)*

7. In view of his method of working, what do you think may have helped him discover this unified space? *(his practice of arranging figures in a box and then drawing and painting them)*

8. We can identify a key aspect of linear perspective by finding the point where all the converging lines would meet. Using a ruler and a black-and-white copy of this painting of the Queen of Sheba, trace all the converging lines until you find the vanishing point. Where is it? *(It is in the center of the archway, just above the water.)*

9. Where is Solomon's eye level compared to the vanishing point? *(It is slightly above it, even with the top of the arch.)*

10. Where is the eye level of the queen? *(It is slightly below the vanishing point.)*

11. If the vanishing point identifies where my eyes are as I view this picture, what can I conclude about my position? *(I am a little above the pavement where everyone else is standing and a little below Solomon; I am looking down on the scene.)*

Understanding and Evaluating (pp. 112-14)

Questions and Answers

1. Look again at I Kings 10:1-13. Compare the story to the picture, listing the details that are found in the Scripture and in the painting. *(The details provided in Scripture make up a "great train" and include camels, spices, gold, and precious stones. The details in the painting include servants, gold vessels, and ivory tusks.)*

2. Note the kinds of things she listed in his palace (v. 5). *(She noted his house, his food, the sitting of his servants, the attendants of his ministers and their apparel, the cupbearers, and the stairway ascending to the house of the Lord.)*

3. The following riddles come from the Jewish Targums about the story of the Queen of Sheba. See if you can figure them out. *(Students will probably have difficulty figuring these out.)*

   A. A cistern of wood,
      buckets of iron;
      they draw up stones;
      they cause water to flow. *(Kohl, a powder used for eyeliner, was stored in a reed. To apply it, the user took a small rod of metal, dipped it in water, and lined the eye with the paste. The black line was supposed to make the eye look larger and was usually extended considerably beyond the corner of the eye. You can see an example in the portrait head of Nefertiti. Of course, if the makeup got into the eye, it would cause tears.)*

B. [Like] dust it comes forth from the earth;
   It is nourished from the dust of earth;
   It is poured out like water;
   It illumines the house. *(naphtha, a clear, flowing mineral oil that was used in lamps to light the houses)*

4. Which story do you think Tintoretto was following? Why do you think so? *(the biblical one; none of the Targum details are present)*

5. Why do you think artists working for a church would paint a story about which so little is known? *(Its importance in traditional church art was its prefiguring of the story of the Magi coming to visit the baby Jesus.)*

6. Examine the painting to find and list examples of the features listed above. *(Ladies at the left have high-waisted dresses with low necklines and contrasting belts; the queen's dress drags on the ground; several ladies have uncovered heads, which show their hair; the woman in front and the queen both have braided hair; one woman at the left has a hat that looks like a cone on her head, and another has one that looks like feathers; the man at the right has a turban.)*

7. From what has been said about Tintoretto's art, what do you think the new problem was? *(how to make the figures dramatically interact within a deep space)*

8. What answers did he find for this problem? *(using consistent linear perspective and leaving enough space for figures; using little figurines in a box to plan his paintings; moving at least one figure close to the picture plane so that the viewers feel that they are in the picture too; putting the horizon or eye-level line where it identifies the viewers' location in the picture)*

Creative Expression Lessons

Lesson one: Fashion and time

Materials needed
- old magazines and catalogs
- banner paper or bulletin board paper
- staples or another method for hanging the pictures

Objective
The students will do the following:
- Collect pictures from old magazines or catalogs or make copies from books and group them according to time period

Procedure (p. 115)
1. Collect any old magazines or catalogs. If these are valuable, make copies of pictures. Try to collect materials that cover the last several decades.

2. Collect pictures of fashions from these sources. Advertisements are a good source. Date the fashion by the date of publication or by information given in the magazine or book.

3. Assemble your fashion pictures into a time line on a bulletin board or banner paper. Mark the dates below the pictures.

4. You may wish to include objects like cars or utensils along with the fashions on your time line.

5. You may also include current events from that time.

Assessment
- Play time travel detective. Describe a character you are trying to find. Include details of clothing and perhaps references to current events and issues in your clues. Students must try to identify the approximate time period described.

Lesson two: One-point linear perspective

Materials needed
- white drawing paper, 12" × 18"
- rulers
- pencils
- masking tape
- T-square
- colored pencils or pointed water-based markers
- projector markers and a small T-square for use with an overhead projector
- overhead projector

Objective
The students will do the following:
- Work out an accurate diagram of perspective space

Procedure (pp. 115-16)
1. Position a 12" × 18" piece of drawing paper horizontally on your desk.

2. Using a ruler, divide the bottom edge of the paper into equal units and mark the measurements.

3. Use that same measurement to find the horizon line five units up from the bottom of the paper. Tintoretto used a measure about one-fifth of a man's height as a handy division for pavement squares. That way he could easily calculate how much space was between any two points in the drawing. Mark the horizon line on the right and left sides of the paper and draw it all the way across the paper.

4. Measure on the horizon line to find the exact center of the paper; place a dot there. That will become the vanishing point for the perspective.

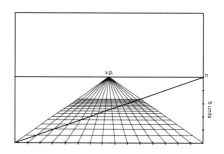

5. Now connect the marks at the bottom edge of the paper with the vanishing point so that they all converge in the center.

6. Use the ruler to draw a diagonal line from the bottom left corner of the paper to the place where the horizon line touches the right edge of the paper. Where this line crosses each converging line, there will be a horizontal division.

7. Tape your paper on the desk in a horizontal position using a T-square to keep it straight. With the T-square hooked over the edge of the desk, draw the horizontal divisions. Now you have a pavement of squares, each one-fifth the size of a man, receding into the distance.

8. Use either colored pencils or pointed markers to color in every other square.

Assessments

• Demonstrate the process step-by-step using projector markers and a ruler on an overhead projector.

• Walk around to observe which students seem to understand what they are doing. The next lesson will continue this project.

Lesson three: Constructing a scene

Materials needed

• old magazines and catalogs
• scissors
• perspective drawings from Lesson two
• glue stick
• waxed paper
• heavy books (to be used as weights)

Objectives

The students will do the following:

• Cut out a number of figures and other objects from magazine pictures
• Paste their figures and objects into a collage

Procedure (p. 116)

1. Use old magazines and catalogs to find figures you can cut out. Try to find one large figure and a variety of other sizes of figures. Cut them out carefully around the edges of all shapes so that none of the background shows.

2. Also find and cut out scenery, buildings, cars, and any other objects that might fit into the scene.

3. Lay your cutouts on the paper in their proper positions. Remember that the horizon represents your eye level. Place all objects on the paper according to where they would be in relation to your eye level. For example, a house would have about one-half of its first story below the eye level and the other half above.

4. People should be placed so that their eyes are on the eye-level line unless they are clearly shorter than an adult, such as children.

5. Continue to search for and cut out other elements that will make an interesting scene. Use trees, bushes, and flowers to hide the bare paper at each side of the squared pavement.

6. When you have all the pieces you need, start gluing from the back to the front, overlapping near objects over more distant ones. Glue pieces thoroughly so that the edges will not curl up.

7. Lay waxed paper over the collage; then stack all of the collages on top of one another with waxed paper in between them and weight the stack down with books overnight to flatten them.

Assessments

• Have the students describe their location and tell what is going on. You may also want to have them write a short story about the people in their scene.

• Evaluate the collage based on the illusion of fairly convincing space created by the objects, their size, and their placement on the perspective lines.

Lesson four: Drawing objects in two-point perspective

Materials needed

• white drawing paper, 12" × 18"
• rulers
• pencils

Objective

The students will do the following:

• Find the two vanishing points and construct a city scene

Procedure (p. 117)

1. With a 12" × 18" piece of drawing paper positioned horizontally on your desk, measure and draw a horizon or eye-level line. If you want your city to appear as though you are standing on the ground looking up at it, draw the line near the bottom. If you want it to look as though you are viewing the scene from the middle floors of a skyscraper, draw the line in the middle. If you want the effect of flying over the city, draw the line very near the top.

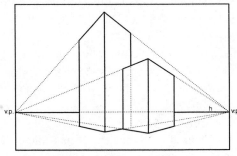

Looking up at the city from a low point of view

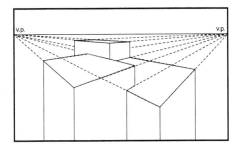

2. Place the two vanishing points as close as possible to the outside edges of the paper, on the horizon line.

3. All the lines that are vertical will still remain vertical, but all other lines will point toward one of the vanishing points. The height of the structures will depend on the length of the vertical line you make.

4. Start each building with a vertical line that represents the corner closest to you. From the top of the line, draw a slanting line toward one of the vanishing points. Lines that recede to the right will aim toward the point at the right; lines that recede toward the left will point to the left vanishing point. From the bottom of the vertical line, draw another line toward the same vanishing point. Choose where you want the back of the building to be and draw a vertical line there. The shape can be seen as either a trapezoid or a rectangle receding away from you. Draw the other side the same way, but use the opposite vanishing point.

5. Working from front to back, continue to draw more buildings the same way that you drew this first one. Keep in mind that all lines except the vertical ones will point to one or the other vanishing point. Use a variety of sizes and challenging relationships between buildings.

6. Optional: Add windows and doors and other architectural features to turn the boxes into buildings.

Assessment

• Evaluate the perspective drawing for complexity, creativity in adding individual details and challenging forms, and understanding of form shown by consistent use of vanishing points and shading or color value. In a drawing like this, neatness is also important.

Chapter 10: *The Drama of Art*

Seeing and Perceiving (pp. 123-25)

Questions and Answers

The Holy Family in the Carpenter Shop

1. Is there a Scripture verse from which this subject was taken? *(no)*

2. What is happening in the picture? *(Young Jesus and Mary are helping Joseph in his shop.)*

3. In addition to the title, are there any indications that these people are Joseph, Mary, and Jesus? *(They have very faint halos over their heads.)*

4. What class of people do they look like? *(They are blue-collar or working-class people.)* Why do you think so? *(They are wearing plain clothes; the face of Joseph is weatherworn; the surroundings are rustic; upper-class people did not do carpentry work.)*

5. What time is it? *(It is sometime after sunset; it is dark inside.)*

6. What is the source of the light? *(The light source is the little lamp held by Jesus.)*

7. What effects do you see in the picture that indicate that this is the only source of light? *(The shadow of the lamp and the shadow of Mary's arm indicate that this is the only source of light; also the shadows are all on the opposite side from the lamp, and the brightest highlights are close to the lamp; dimmer ones are farther away.)*

8. How much space is there in this room? *(There seems to be just a few feet of space; it is hard to tell exactly since the wall is in the shadows.)*

9. Name one aspect of *The Holy Family* that illustrates each method from the preceding paragraph. *(Jesus is right at the front; His arm sticks out almost past the frame; He is holding the only light in the picture and His arm is shadowed on the table top; there is an especially strong contrast on Joseph's arm; Joseph's face has deep furrows; the painting is almost neutral, dark colors, but Mary's dress has intense red; Jesus is the repoussoir figure, and there is a table; everybody is very close to the table, and there is not much space around the edges.)*

Esther Accusing Haman

10. How is it different from *The Holy Family*? *(It looks as though rich people live here—the clothes are much fancier; it does not look like Bible times because of the clothes; the light does not come from a candle.)*

11. How far back is the most distant object in this room? *(It is five to seven feet to the curtain behind Ahasuerus;*

there is a balcony you can see at the left that is farther away.)

12. Are we looking down at this scene or up at it, or are we on the same level as the three people? *(We are on the same level as Esther, above Haman, and below the king.)*

13. Look at the textures in the painting. How many materials can you identify in the painting by their texture? *(glass, silver, dough, satin, ermine, velvet, fringe, pearls and gold, skin, etc.)*

14. Which do you feel was probably more important to this painter: making a convincing three-dimensional space with three-dimensional people in it or creating realistic textures? *(probably the textures)*

15. Do the figures seem three-dimensional? *(Yes, but the texture is what you notice first.)*

16. What is the source of light in the room? How can you tell where it is coming from? *(We cannot see the source; it may be a window at the left; it is too bright for candles, however, so it must be daylight. We can tell it is coming from the left because the lightest parts are on that side and the darkest shadows are on the right.)*

17. How near is the window? *(The window must be fairly close judging from the amount of light that falls on Esther.)*

18. There is one other source of light—the little balcony at the left. If you wanted to go from the dining room to that balcony, how would you get there? *(It is not actually clear, but it looks as though you would have to go down some stairs.)*

Understanding and Evaluating (p. 126)

Questions and Answers

1. What moral could Honthorst's painting have? *(the value of family togetherness, the value and dignity of hard work; perseverance—it is after dark and they are still working; the possibility of overcoming a poor background)*

2. Which one of the men is Ahasuerus and which is Haman? *(Ahasuerus is standing; Haman is seated at the right.)*

3. Read Esther 7:1-6. What exact moment has Victors represented? *(He is representing verse 6, when Esther reveals the source of the plot.)*

4. How does Ahasuerus respond? *(He stands; also his face looks as if he is growing angry.)*

5. He extends a hand to each of the other two people at the table. What does each hand gesture communicate? *(His gesture toward Esther is gentle and comforting; his gesture toward Haman is a fist.)*

6. Where is Haman looking? *(toward Esther)*

7. What is Haman's reaction to Ahasuerus? *(He is afraid. He seems to be pushing his chair back as if he is considering running away.)*

8. Where does the story take place? Do the clothes and furnishings look appropriate to that part of the world? If not, what part of the world would you say these clothes represent? *(The story takes place in Persia, but the clothes and furnishings look European—perhaps the Dutch idea of what royalty might wear. Remember that the Dutch had been ruled by Spanish kings.)*

9. Victors tries to make the clothes look exotic and foreign. Can you find one detail to show this? *(Esther's crown)*

10. Aside from illustrating the Old Testament story, can you think of a moral that Victors might have had in mind when he painted Esther? *(Answers will vary. Knowing the historical background, however, he may have been warning against political corruption.)*

Creative Expression Lessons

Lesson one: Drawing objects

Materials needed
- still-life objects
- #2 pencils
- newsprint
- clear acrylic sheet, 11" × 14" (optional)

Objective
The students will do the following:
- Draw individual still-life objects with correct proportions and shapes

Procedure (p. 127)
1. Your teacher, perhaps with your help, will assemble a collection of still-life objects such as vases, dishes, bottles, fruit, shells, leaves, candlesticks, bouquets of silk flowers, interesting cloth, old books, and any other objects with interesting texture or form.

2. Choose one object at a time and begin to study its shape. You can do this by tracing its edges aerially: close one eye and place the point of your pencil where it seems to touch the edge of the object. The pencil will never actually touch the object, but its point should look as though it does. Run the pencil around the edge of the object several times, keeping the pencil approximately the same distance from your face all the time.

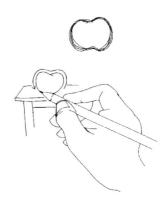

3. After the aerial tracing, put the pencil on the paper and draw the same outline while looking at the still-life object. If you have trouble doing the aerial tracing, hold a piece of clear acrylic sheet in front of you and trace the edges with your finger on the acrylic and then draw it on the paper.

4. Several of these shape and proportion studies should be done in short sessions of five or ten minutes each. When you have gained confidence in the representation of a single object, choose your best one to hang up in front of the class. Your class will choose those that have the best proportion and most accurate shape in representing the object.

5. Choose another object that you have not yet drawn, perhaps a more complex one, and do a more detailed drawing of it with many details you did not have time to include on the short drawings.

Assessment
- Have each student do a self-evaluation of his work.

Lesson two: Shading

Materials needed
- old objects such as balls, wooden objects, old turned furniture legs, inexpensive vases or statuary, flower pots, and so on
- white or gray spray paint
- portable floodlights with reflector shades and clamps
- white drawing paper
- soft drawing pencils (2B or 3B) or soft charcoal pencils

Objective
The students will do the following:
- Shade the objects, representing their form and texture

Procedure (p. 128)
1. You will help your teacher collect old objects and spray paint several of them white or gray to cover up the natural texture, colors, or designs on the surface. Use the spray paint outdoors and avoid breathing the overspray.

2. Set up several objects with a floodlight shining on them to create a raking light. If floodlights are unavailable, put the still lifes near a window and turn out the overhead lighting.

3. Draw one or two of the objects and shade them to show their three-dimensional form. Use at least four different values: highlight, light, shadow, and reflected light. Practice several times from different points of view.

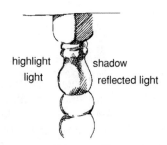

highlight   shadow
light   reflected light

4. When you are shading the form of the object well, choose objects that have not been painted. Shade the form only, ignoring the color, designs, or surface of the object.

5. Finally, draw objects, shade the form, and then add the colors, textures, and patterns that appear on the surface. If the objects are losing their three-dimensional form because of too much detail, go back to shading form alone.

6. Place your best drawings on the bulletin board, choosing those that show the most convincing form and that best combine the form with the surface appearance of the object.

Note: Each student should do many drawings over a week's time with several self-evaluations or class evaluations.

Assessments
- Divide the class into small groups and perform a group evaluation of the students' work.
- Following the group evaluation, do your own evaluation of the students' work.

Lesson three: Still life

Materials needed
- still-life objects
- cloths to drape behind objects
- small tables or three-sided boxes
- portable floodlights with reflector shades and clamps
- white drawing paper
- soft drawing pencils (2B or 3B) or soft charcoal pencils
- waxy black-colored pencils

Objectives
The students will do the following:

- Select and arrange objects in a good composition with a center of interest and with objects that overlap
- Draw the still life and shade at least the center of interest

Procedure (pp. 128-29)
1. Your teacher will divide the class into groups of five or six students each.

2. From the number of objects assembled, choose several objects to make into a still life. Choose objects with a variety of shapes and textures. Drape a cloth behind them. Still lifes can be set up on small tables or inside a portable wooden box with three sides.

3. Pay attention to good composition as you choose and set up your still lifes: have a center of interest, use a variety of heights, overlap items to show their relation in space, and arrange objects and folds of the cloth to create lines that lead into the composition.

4. Set up floodlights so that the still lifes are illuminated from one side and above. If floodlights are unavailable, put the still lifes near a window and turn out the overhead lighting.

5. Choose a point of view and draw the still life. Begin with light sketches to place objects. As the drawing progresses, darken the lines.

6. Begin shading some areas. Do not shade too darkly to begin with since it is easier to darken an area than to lighten one. If you use waxy black-colored pencils, the shading will not smear and the finished work will be neater; or use a cover sheet under your hand while working.

7. Begin in the focal point area: it will take a long time to finish; you may need to leave background areas partially unfinished. Sometimes a drawing is more interesting if not all of it is shaded equally.

Assessments
- Have the students first do a self-evaluation of still-life setup.
- Do a class evaluation in mid-project.
- When the projects are complete, do your own evaluation of each student's work.

Chapter 11: The Colonial and the King

Seeing and Perceiving (p. 137)

Questions and Answers

The Brazen Serpent

1. In which of the three styles above does it fit? *(It fits the Dread Mode.)* Why do you think so? *(The violent action, three-dimensional space, emotional faces, and strong emotions shown reflect the style.)*

2. How far back in space does the scene extend? *(about ten feet)* What is behind the figures? *(We cannot tell for sure—light, a cloud perhaps.)* Why did the artist not include a beautiful background landscape? *(He wanted to focus our attention on the action, to prevent our getting distracted by the background, and to focus more strongly on the emotion.)*

3. Look at the lines in the painting. What kinds of lines do you see most—vertical and horizontal or diagonal and curving? *(diagonal and curving)*

4. Make a photocopy of the painting with the copier at its lightest setting. Turn the copy upside down and look at the patterns of light and dark. What happens to the unity of the picture? *(It breaks up into little bits of light and dark that are all mixed together. It is hard to see the individual figures.)*

Esau and Jacob Presented to Isaac

5. Now look at the painting *Esau and Jacob Presented to Isaac.* How are the two paintings alike? *(Both deal with an Old Testament subject; the figures have simple robes; there is a lot of light and dark contrast.)*

6. How are they different? *(Esau and Jacob Presented to Isaac is much calmer; it has less emotion, less movement, more unity, and deeper space in the background.)*

Understanding and Evaluating (pp. 138-40)

Questions and Answers

1. What might be some of the emotions you and others would feel? List as many as you can. *(fear, anger, dismay, pity, confusion, faith, acceptance, repentance, sorrow, terror, etc.)* How many of these emotions can you identify in the people in the picture? *(Answers will vary.)*

2. What pictorial devices has the artist used to create this heroic figure? *(Moses is the only figure shown completely; all others are partially overlapped. The artist silhouettes the head and arm of Moses against light so that he stands out. All the other figures form a massive pile under his feet. People look and gesture toward him.)*

3. Do you think sympathy would be important to today's aesthetician? Why or why not? *(Modern aestheticians tend to treat art as though it is purely a matter of colors, lines, shapes, and so on, unrelated to all other values such as emotion, morality, responsibility, or belief.)*

Creative Expression Lessons

Lesson one: Study of human proportions

Materials needed
- white drawing paper
- #2 pencils
- rulers
- large size roll of butcher paper or white wrapping paper
- newsprint
- Bristol board or tag board (one 5" × 10" piece per student)
- scissors
- short pieces of crayon (medium to dark colors) with paper removed

Objectives
The students will do the following:
- Study generic proportions for the adult human figure and compare actual students to the proportions
- Draw and cut parts for the figure, arrange parts in a pose, and do a crayon rubbing

Procedure (pp. 140-41)
1. Make a chart showing generic human proportions.

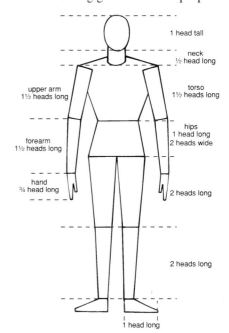

2. Your teacher will choose two students, one who is short and lightly built and another who is tall or husky. Each one will lie down on a large piece of butcher paper or newsprint. Another student will outline with a pencil, following fairly closely the contours of the student lying down. When both students have been outlined, compare their proportions to the generic chart to see whether they differ.

3. Draw the various portions of the body on a sheet of heavy paper or card stock about ten inches high following the proportions on the chart. Cut them out with scissors.

4. Lay the parts together, overlapping joints and bending them to create different poses. Experiment with various poses. When you have found one you like, arrange the figure in place on a piece of newsprint.

5. Lay a thin piece of white paper over the figure. Hold it with one hand. Lay a piece of peeled crayon flat on the paper and rub over the cut paper. The edges will show up as dark lines. Keep rubbing until you have revealed all the shapes under the paper. Expand the idea by rearranging your figure several times and doing multiple crayon rubbings in different colors. You may arrange the figures like a multiple exposure of a single action or like a group of people. Your teacher may have several students work together to arrange their figures in a group action. Props can be cut out of the same paper.

Assessment
- Check the proportion of their action figures and evaluate the picture for proportion, neatness, and convincing poses.

Lesson two: Expressions of emotion

Materials needed
- old magazines or newspapers
- newsprint
- #2 pencils
- erasers
- white drawing paper

Objectives
The students will do the following:
- Select a pose that shows a specific emotion
- Sketch a figure in that pose

Procedure (p. 141)
1. Your teacher will lead a class discussion on the way body position and gestures convey emotion. Your teacher will then have several students adopt positions while others guess what emotions they are portraying.

2. Select an emotion to portray. Decide what pose the person would adopt to express that emotion. You may role-play or have others model for you. You may use old magazines to look for pictures also. Use whole body gestures, not facial expressions.

3. Practice balloon sketching the actions, using freely drawn ovals to represent body parts. Apply what you know about proportion to this sketch.

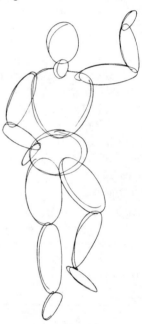

4. Refine the sketch by erasing extra lines and adding clothing and other details to complete the drawing. You may want to refine the sketch by tracing only the outlines onto another piece of paper and finishing the drawing.

Assessments
- Demonstrate and assist the students in sketching with ovals, keeping natural proportions.
- Evaluate the drawing for communication of emotion, proportion, use of imagination, and neatness.

Lesson three: Adding drama

Materials needed
- old news magazines or newspapers
- newsprint
- #2 pencils
- erasers
- scissors
- glue sticks or paper paste
- white drawing paper
- drawing pencils, 2B or 3B

Objectives
The students will do the following:
- Find a newspaper photo of an exciting event
- Identify a key figure from this event, create a dramatic pose for him or her, and rearrange other figures to create a dramatic climax

Procedure (p. 141)
1. Look for newspaper or magazine pictures of an exciting event. The picture should include close-up views of people.
2. Study the photo and read its caption. Find the person who seems to you to be a key figure in the story. Consider what emotions the person would be feeling at this moment. Change the pose so that it more dramatically expresses the feeling. Sketch and then refine the figure as you did in Lesson two.
3. Carefully cut around the edges of the other figures and rearrange them around the key figure so that they build up a dramatic climax around the key person. Paste them down. Fill in spaces in between the pieces of photo by drawing.
4. Retrace the picture using your new arrangement. Correct poses and proportions as needed. Move your tracing sheet when necessary to rearrange parts of the picture.
5. Choose a light source, preferably from one side, and shade the picture according to the light source. Use a full range of grays from black to white with at least three values in between. A soft pencil will make a better range of grays.

Assessments
- Observe and discuss the students' choices of their key figures.
- Evaluate their composition for correct proportion, drama, placement of figures, imagination, and light source.

Lesson four: Experimenting with color

Materials needed
- medium-sized watercolor brushes (student grade)
- transparent watercolors (one tube each of yellow ocher, burnt sienna or Indian red, Prussian blue, alizarin crimson, cadmium yellow light, and cerulean blue)
- Styrofoam plates for palettes
- white drawing paper
- a sample color wheel (optional)

Objectives
The students will do the following:
- Experiment with the same colors Benjamin West claimed to use as a child
- Paint a color wheel with twelve colors mixed from the primary colors

Procedure (p. 142)
1. To approximate the colors Benjamin West claimed to have painted with, use yellow ocher, burnt sienna or Indian red, and Prussian blue watercolor or gouache. Try mixing the secondary colors. What kinds of colors did you get?
2. Now use alizarin crimson, cadmium yellow light, and cerulean blue. Mix the secondaries again. What kinds of colors did you get this time? The colors in the second set more closely resemble the actual wavelengths of light from the sun.
3. Your teacher will explain the color wheel and demonstrate the process of mixing and placing colors on it. Paint the primary colors directly from the tube, mix secondaries, and paint them. Mix all the intermediate colors and paint them. The result will be a color wheel with twelve hues: three primaries, three secondaries, and six intermediates.

Assessments
- Have students describe the colors they mix.
- Evaluate the color wheels for accuracy in mixing and placement of colors and for neatness of painting.

Chapter 12: Gustave Doré, the Sublime and Sentimental

Seeing and Perceiving (pp. 150-52)

Questions and Answers

The Ascension

1. Look at the reproduction of *The Ascension*. What trait in this painting represents romanticism? *(facial expressions and gestures)*

2. Compare the painting to Doré's engraving of the same subject. Which is more emotional in character? Why do you think so? *(The painting is more emotional; the engraving focuses more on gestures, but the painting focuses on faces.)*

3. In the engraving, what kinds of reactions can we see in the disciples? *(We can see awe, amazement, fear, and even protest; some of them look as though they are trying to call Him back.)*

4. What are the reactions of the angels in the painting? *(We see pity, sympathy, and sorrow in the angels' expressions.)*

5. Look at the etching. If you were actually present at this event, where would you be standing? *(on the ground with the disciples)*

6. Where would you be in the painted scene? *(in the sky with the angels)*

7. What is your station point in the painting? *(Our station point is a little lower than Christ's head, near the middle of the picture. It is hard to determine since the clouds hide the horizon line.)*

8. How has the artist created this effect? *(He has done so by spreading the landscape out below the viewer and hiding the horizon line.)*

9. Before the invention of airplanes, how would an artist know what the ground looked like from up in the air? *(Doré's mountain-hiking experiences would have helped him.)*

10. Doré also experimented with another contemporary idea in painting: working en plein air. Can you see a difference in painting style between the landscape and the figures of the angels? *(Yes. The landscape has a more solid, realistic look; the angels look more artificial or invented, more romantic.)*

11. Doré always liked to include movement in his work. What is the direction of the movement in this painting? *(The direction of the movement is from the disciples' feet diagonally upward toward the bright light at the top, the heavens.)*

12. How did the artist create this sense of movement? *(He did so by the size and direction of the bodies and by the limited contrast of value and color in the distance.)*

13. A device artists use frequently to portray distance in a painting is to place a repoussoir figure at the front of the picture. That figure establishes the near boundary of the scene by showing the distance between the nearest and farthest objects in the picture. Can you see a figure used like that in each of these pictures? *(the disciples at the left in the engraving and the angels at the left and right in the painting)*

14. Although we might be tempted to call this painting realistic, Doré chose the colors to create an effect. He used warm colors and analogous colors in the angels to contrast with the strong, cool color of Christ's robe. Why do you think he chose those colors? *(He chose those colors to remind us of heaven [gold], to make Christ stand out clearly, and to provide a contrast with the earth.)*

Understanding and Evaluating (p. 153)

Questions and Answers

1. What this critic disliked seems now to be one of Doré's strong points: he interpreted. He used every detail of a composition to help interpret his story. Look at the position of Christ in the painted *Ascension*. What does it mean? *(Christ's positioning is similar to His position on the cross.)*

2. What does the small landscape add to this picture? *(The landscape provides separation from the disciples; having finished the task, Christ is returning to heaven. The landscape puts Him back into His proper realm.)*

3. Doré's painting is actually an illustration, not a painting at all. Based on your general knowledge of the two terms *illustration* and *painting*, how would you explain the differences between the two? *(Your students' general knowledge of the two terms* painting *and* illustration *should enable them to draw some general conclusions. However, you may need to guide them in discerning the following specific distinctions. Illustration expresses the meaning of a story and takes the point of view of the author; painting expresses the experiences and point of view primarily of the artist. Illustration contains details that illuminate the story; enjoyment of the illustration is based on knowing something about the story. Enjoyment of a painting depends on the qualities of artistry of the painting. A good painting can be enjoyed even if you do not know*

the story. Illustration serves a goal outside itself; painting serves primarily the goal of visual enjoyment and expression of common experiences.)

4. Looking back at what you have read about his life and times, give at least one reason he failed to achieve that goal. *(Student answers will vary, but some ideas include the lack of proper training, too much early success, overprotective mother, too little commitment and self-sacrifice for art, too much craving for popularity and success, too much dependence on his talent, and the unpopularity of religious art except in England.)*

5. How might his life have been different if he had broken away from his doting mother? *(Maybe he would have been more willing to take chances and try new things.)*

6. How might it have been different if his mother had never received an inheritance? *(He would have had to continue to work to get through school; perhaps he might have met and joined the more creative artists of his time.)*

7. How might it have been different if he had not been part of upper-class society? *(He might have had less pressure to remain popular; he might have been freer to do the things his instinct told him to do.)*

8. Name some pros and cons of contentment in the life of an artist like Doré. *(Pros might include the following: he was content with his situation in life; he seems to have held life-long friendships. Some cons might include the following: he mistook financial success and popularity for artistic success; he was too content with his family's praise and encouragement; he was content with his social life and lost sight of a larger goal.)*

9. Is contentment always good? or always bad? When is it good or bad? *(It is good if we are content with what we cannot change—God's will and surrounding circumstances that we cannot control. It is bad if we are content with our own performance, particularly if we are just beginning or have not tried very hard. Contentment with a low goal may produce a temporary feeling of self-worth, but in the long run it disappoints. One of the requirements for success is the willingness to set aside the good to achieve the best. Paul prayed for the Philippian Christians, "that your love may abound yet more and more in knowledge and in all judgment; That ye may approve things that are excellent" [Phil. 1:9-10].)*

Note: You may want to compare Doré's *Ascension* painting with *The Crucifixion* by Peter Paul Rubens. Rubens's work can be found in many art history books. The original art piece is also discussed in the video *The Glories of Baroque: Flemish, Dutch, Spanish, and French Painting* (available from BJU Press). In your comparison, point out that

Rubens's figure is stronger and more three-dimensional, the space seems deeper, and there is less emotion.

Creative Expression Lessons

Lesson one: Developing a sketchbook

Materials needed
- spiral-bound drawing pad, about 9" × 12", or sheets of white drawing paper in a notebook
- #2 pencils

Objective
The students will do the following:
- Start a sketchbook

Procedure (p. 154)
1. Buy or make a sketchbook of blank white drawing paper. List specific items you might need to be able to draw to be an illustrator. Your list should contain people as well as various objects, animals, and possibly places.

2. Establish a regular schedule for adding drawings to your sketchbook and for checking it regularly. Make a list of specific subjects to study, such as hands, faces, or facial expressions. Draw your own picture from a mirror. Draw people of all ages. Draw animals. Always draw from real objects, never from photographs or other drawings. If you imitate photographs and other artists' drawings, you will never learn how to draw by yourself.

3. Look in a library and list some books and magazine articles to read that discuss art, artists, art history, art techniques, or art museums. Write regular reading reports in the sketchbook or another notebook.

4. Keep a journal that includes your notes on planning sketches and the artwork you are working on.

Assessments
- Check the students' lists to make sure they listed a variety of items and that some of them are detail studies of the human figure.
- Make a regular schedule for checking student sketchbooks. Check them for the number and quality of drawings of assigned topics. Write notes and make suggestions in the sketchbook. Check their reading lists, perhaps providing additional sources for them. Read students' reports. When they hand in artwork, check the notes about it in the sketchbook.

Lesson two: Using your sketches

Materials needed
- several children's stories
- sketchbook
- #2 pencils
- fine-line pens

Objective
The students will do the following:
- Illustrate a specific episode of a story

Procedure (p. 154)

1. Look through children's books for a story and pick a specific episode of that story to illustrate.

2. Decide what you will need to draw and work on a series of sketches of objects, parts of the body, settings, and so forth. Draw several different points of view of each item. Try drawing objects from memory. If you forget part of the object, glance at it and then put it away again.

3. Sketch quickly a rough plan of the illustration. Decide where each item will be. Remember how the horizon line helped Doré establish a station point for his illustrations? Decide what point of view you want of the scene. Sometimes an unusual point of view is effective, such as Doré's angel-eye view. Plan the light source and where shadows should fall.

4. Consult your sketches but do not trace or copy them. Make the final drawing a completely new drawing using what you learned from the sketches. Shade the drawing according to the light source. If you wish, you may make another version using ink. A fine-line pen makes a good sketching tool. Make darker values by cross hatching.

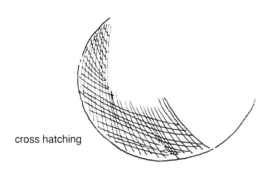

cross hatching

Assessments

- Check the students' sketches in their sketchbooks and make suggestions.

- Have each student read his story or episode to the class, explaining what he has included and why.

- Evaluate the finished illustration against the sketchbook, looking for solid three-dimensionality, composition that communicates the episode, and convincing light and shade. If this is a project they kept journal notes on, read the journal and give encouragement and helpful suggestions.

Lesson three: Scratchboard drawings

Materials needed

- Bristol board, poster board, or scratchboard
- black crayon
- crushed chalk or cornstarch
- black India ink
- still-life objects
- newsprint
- #2 pencils
- desk light
- white chalkboard chalk
- masking tape
- kitchen paring knives or scratchboard tool (You may wish to cover all but ½" of the paring knife blade with masking tape.)

Objective

The students will do the following:

- Make a scratchboard drawing

Procedure (p. 155)

1. Use a piece of Bristol board or poster board for the base. Commercially prepared scratchboard is also available. (Paper is too thin and will curl and tear.) The board should have a smooth, coated surface. Color the surface heavily with black crayon, pressing hard enough so that streaks do not show. Powder the surface of the crayon with crushed chalk or cornstarch. Brush black India ink over the powder to coat the whole board. Set it aside to dry.

2. Choose a single still-life object. Place it in front of you and draw on paper its outlines and interior contours. Darken the room and place a desk light to illuminate one side of the object. Shade the object, showing the gradual change from light to dark around the curved sides. Do not try to reproduce pictures, patterns, or writing on the object, though.

3. When the scratchboard is completely dry, trace the outlines of your drawing onto the surface. To do this, rub white chalk on the back of your drawing. Shake off the excess chalk. Turn the drawing chalk-side down and tape it to the front of the board. With a pencil, trace over the outlines only. When the chalked drawing is removed, there will be a chalk line on the scratchboard. Using the point of a kitchen paring knife or a scratchboard knife, gently scrape away the dark coating, showing the white paper underneath. Be careful not to tear the paper. Scratchboard drawing works just like ink drawing but in reverse. Now you will represent highlights by cross hatching. Represent the same gradual change from dark to light by scratching away more and more of the black coating as you go toward the light. Try several small areas, about three inches square, before you try a big area.

Assessment

- Evaluate the finished scratchboard drawing for a gradual change of values from light to dark and for reasonably correct proportions. (If students have excessive trouble shading, try getting old objects and spray painting them white. [See Chapter 10, Lesson two.] Without the natural color to confuse them, students will be better able to see the values.)

Chapter 13:

Seeing and Perceiving (pp. 161-63)

Questions and Answers

Wittenburg, October 31, 1517

1. We do not know whether this tag was placed on the painting by its creator or somebody else, but such long explanations were often displayed with history paintings. Why do you suppose long labels were used? *(Long labels were used probably because people would enjoy the specific details of the event or because otherwise they might not know what the painting was about.)*

2. Knowing what is happening, what details did the artist include that show us the specific event? *(He included a Gothic-looking church, Luther in his medieval robes with a hammer in hand, some soldiers, some monks and a nun, and so on.)*

3. Crowe included several specific characters in his painting: John Tetzel, Luther's father and mother, Catherine von Bora, and Lucas Cranach. Your teacher will divide the class into groups. Use encyclopedias and books on sixteenth-century church history to read about the day when Luther posted his theses on the church door. Search for information on the people mentioned above. Report to the class on what you find. *(Findings will vary.)*

Note: The Triumph of Truth: A Life of Martin Luther by J. H. Merle D'Aubigne, edited by Mark Sidwell, is an excellent source of information on the life of Martin Luther. (Available from BJU Press)

4. Can you find the picture of John Tetzel? *(John Tetzel was a Dominican monk who had been selling indulgences since 1501. We can see him to the left in his Dominican robes, riding on the horse [or is it a mule?], clutching his money box.)*

5. Can you find Catherine von Bora? Does Crowe's picture of her look like this portrait? *(Catherine von Bora was a nun who escaped from the convent and eventually married Luther. She is to the right in the foreground. Crowe's picture does look a little like the portrait.)*

6. Which figures do you think may represent Luther's parents? Why? *(Luther's parents were Hans and Grethe Luther—stern, rigorous peasant people; they are on the right side of the painting. Crowe seems to have added a younger sister.)*

7. What do you think Luther's father is thinking about? What about his mother? *(The father seems to admire his son's courage. The mother is looking worriedly at the crucifix, perhaps wondering if her son is wrong. The daughter looks very scared. Students may have other observations on these people. Allow some discussion.)*

8. How could Crowe have painted portraits of these people over three hundred years after they lived? *(He might have studied Cranach's portraits and the artist's self-portrait.)*

9. Now that you have read about the event, what other details can you find that support the historical accuracy of the painting? *(The building looks like a cathedral; the doors are wooden and have a pointed arch at the top. Tetzel is coming, followed by a crowd that includes several other Dominican friars, a banner, and a crucifix; there are many people around for the festival. Luther was a teacher at the university and is wearing a coat that looks like a graduation gown.)*

10. There are several pilgrims on both sides who have come to town to see the famous relics. There are symbols—scallop shells on their clothes, walking sticks, and canteens—that tell us who they are. Can you find them? *(There are two at the right with shells on their hats; one has a cape with shells. At the left behind Tetzel are two more, one carrying a canteen on a staff.)*

11. There are several people at the right side who seem to be favorable toward Luther. How can you tell? *(They seem to be cheering him on; some have weapons drawn.)*

12. There are two examples of a halberd in the painting. Can you find them? How do you think Crowe would have known about all these details? *(He must have read much about Luther's life.)*

13. Look particularly at the textures in the painting. List the objects that clearly show a realistic visual texture. *(lady's brocade dress, horse's fur, dust, stone wall, wooden doors, and so on)*

14. Who had been carrying it and what has just happened? *(It seems that the first blow has been struck: the flame that will ignite the entire European continent has been lit. It looks as if the papal bull and its elaborate cover were carried by the Dominican monk, who has fled to Tetzel and looks as though he is about to push him off his horse. The soldier in the foreground seems to have knocked the papal bull out of the monk's hands and has his halberd pointed at it. This is an example of hinting at the future events that would result from this single event.)*

15. What might a modern aesthetician think of Eyre Crowe's painting? *(He probably would not like it: too many details, too much storytelling, too little imagination, too photographic, maybe even somewhat melodramatic; notice Tetzel's facial expression.)*

16. Would it also be possible to respond to Crowe's painting or other old masters' paintings according to the "immediate response" theory? In other words, could we just look and immediately enjoy the colors, textures, or composition of this painting even if we did not understand all the details? *(Yes, but it might be harder than it would be with a less photographic effect.)*

17. What artistic elements in the painting do you see and enjoy without having to know the story? *(Even without knowing the story, we can enjoy such details as the variety of colors in the stone wall, the dirt in the street, the way Crowe painted the brocade in the lady's dress in the foreground, and the color of the shadows on the building. Students may have additional opinions.)*

18. Does the average person going to an art gallery respond more like the modern aesthetician, or more like the traditional viewer? Why do you think so? *(He probably responds more like the traditional viewer. He instinctively thinks of the painting as telling a story; he judges painting like literature; he does not look at painting the way an aesthetician does. Students may have other opinions.)*

Understanding and Evaluating (pp. 163-64)

Questions and Answers

1. Look back over what was said about historical narrative painting. According to this standard, is this a good history painting? *(Most students will probably say yes; it has enough details to tell the story and looks very accurate.)*

2. Did Eyre Crowe succeed in making his subject appeal to your imagination in some way? *(Answers will vary; however, they should be supported by explanations.)*

3. The Victorian viewers who originally saw this painting would have appreciated it not only for its historical accuracy but also for the effort that went into it. Does it seem to you that the artist has expended effort in doing his work? *(Yes. Encourage each student to give reasons to support his answer.)*

4. Why do you think he spent his time on history and not genre? *(Maybe he thought it was more important to paint history; maybe he did not realize how much more the genre pictures would be appreciated later; maybe he felt that people could learn more from the history paintings. Students may have other opinions.)*

5. Academic art in general avoided controversial subjects such as religious themes, preferring instead safer subjects that were less likely to be partisan and would

appeal to anybody. Has Eyre Crowe chosen a safe, noncontroversial, pleasant subject for this picture? If not, why do you think this subject might be considered controversial? *(It is a religious subject; even in England there were Catholics who might find the painting offensive. The painting does seem to sympathize with Luther; however, the majority of Victorians were Protestants, and the subject would probably be very popular.)*

Creative Expression Lessons

Lesson one: Visual research

Materials needed
- encyclopedias or books on antiques
- copier
- fine-point markers or roller ball pens with black ink (Tombow or Pigma Micron pens or comparable products)
- white drawing paper
- 4" × 6" cards

Note: Provide some resources or a list of suggested titles to help students in choosing their subjects.

Objective
The students will do the following:
- Research and draw free-hand studies of antique objects

Procedure (pp. 164-65)

1. Make a list of antique weapons and household tools that you find in encyclopedias or collectors' resource books from the library.

2. Choose one object to research. You should find as many pictures as you can of the object, and you may choose to copy them and even enlarge them. Remember that if you enlarge the photograph, you will also enlarge the dot pattern used to print it, and the photograph may be unusable. Use fine pointed markers or roller ball pens to do a finished drawing of the object. Techniques used may include stippling, hatching, and cross-hatching. Your teacher can demonstrate the shading techniques for you and allow you to practice these on scrap paper before trying them on the final drawing. You should not trace the picture in the book nor the copy. Include as much detail as you can.

hatching

3. When you have finished the drawing, write a paragraph on a card about the object and how it was made and used. Include the specific country and dates when it was made. Do not show your classmates the card. Line the drawings up along the wall.

4. Your teacher will either read the cards aloud or distribute them to the students.

5. Try to match the cards with the objects.

Assessments

- Read the students' written paragraphs to check the thoroughness of their information.
- Evaluate the drawings for detail, research, proportion, shading, and neatness.

Lesson two: Drawing a historic character

Materials needed

- books, magazines, encyclopedias
- copier
- #2 pencils
- white drawing paper
- 4" × 6" cards

Objectives

The students will do the following:

- Research a historic character and draw him in historical costume
- Match up the descriptive paragraphs with the drawings as a class activity

Procedure (p. 165)

1. Your teacher may bring in books and magazines or take the class to the library. You should have an idea of what historical person you want to research. You need sources that include pictures of people, costumes, and objects. Books on the history of weapons, objects, and clothing will be useful. Sketch objects you find in the books or photocopy the pictures.

2. Pair up with a classmate so that you can pose for each other. Choose an appropriate pose for the character and the action taking place.

3. Draw your partner, paying particular attention to correct proportion and gesture that you learned in Chapter 11. Trace the drawing, correcting problems with pose or proportion, and then add period costumes. Study and draw the objects the figure might be carrying and add those to the figure. The finished drawing should be at least twelve inches tall. Include all important details but do not put too much emphasis on them. The overall effect should be of one unified figure that looks three-dimensional, not a pile of unrelated details hiding the character.

4. Write a paragraph on a card describing the person you have drawn, when and where he or she lived, and what occupation he or she held. Describe what the person is doing. Do not show your classmates the card. Line the drawings up on a bulletin board or chalkboard.

5. Your teacher will either read the cards aloud or distribute them to the students.

6. Try to match the cards with the appropriate drawings.

Assessments

- Check the drawings to make sure the students have included the necessary costumes and objects.
- Evaluate the drawings for historical accuracy, pose, proportion, and unity. Read each student's paragraph.

Lesson three: Abstract composition conveying conflict

Materials needed

- sheets of construction paper, 9" × 12" (black and white)
- scissors
- glue sticks

Objective

The students will do the following:

- Cut out a number of geometric shapes, arrange them on the opposite color paper, and glue them down

Procedure (pp. 165-66)

1. Take two sheets of 9" × 12" construction paper, one black and one white, and a pair of scissors. Cut out shapes of various sizes and numbers of sides from one of the sheets. Save the other sheet for the background. The design will be more successful if the shapes have a certain unity to them—not just all different ones.

2. Choose an arrangement of shapes to convey the idea of conflict between two groups. Place the shapes on the background paper and begin moving them around until you have a composition that shows conflict. For unity, group the shapes into two or three groups that are in conflict with each other. There will be a focal point or points where the clash is greatest. Several shapes placed close to each other may make one large shape.

3. When the shapes are placed where you want them, glue them down with a glue stick.

Assessments

- Observe and help students decide how to arrange shapes.
- Evaluate the work for unity, conflict, focal point, and neatness.

Chapter 14: Tiffany, Scientist of Light

Seeing and Perceiving (pp. 175-77)

Questions and Answers

St. Paul and Dorcas windows

1. Tracing color *(outlines of face and hands; lettering)*
2. Matte color *(blending of faces and hands)*
3. Plating *(columns at each side; lining of robes)*
4. Drapery glass *(garments)*
5. Jewels *(crowns)*
6. Mottled glass *(trees in background)*
7. Various thicknesses of lead *(around edges and inner contours of garments)*
8. How has the designer created the illusion of space between the figures and the background landscape? *(by using different sizes, overlapping, putting closer objects down farther on the picture plane, and using less detail in the background)*
9. Though he was careful in all other details, the craftsman forgot one piece in the Dorcas window. Can you identify the missing piece? (There should be a back leg showing for the stool on which the sick person is sitting.)

Understanding and Evaluating (pp. 177-78)

Questions and Answers

1. According to that explanation, are Tiffany's windows art nouveau? Why or why not? *(No. There is too much realism and too much three-dimensional space.)*
2. Look at the abstract designs at the top of the panels. Compare them with the picture section itself. What differences do you see? *(The glass at the top is clear instead of opalescent; the design is flat; the color is decorative, more intense, and contains lots of black; nothing there looks realistic.)*
3. Do these two parts of the window seem unified? Why or why not? *(No. There is too much difference in style. Some students may disagree. Evaluate how they support their answers with reasons, not just personal preference.)*
4. Review what you have read about Tiffany's styles. Which of these styles—art nouveau or realist style—do you think he preferred personally? *(He probably preferred art nouveau: the windows he did for exhibitions and for his personal use were all this style.)*

5. Do you remember why he made the realist-style windows? *(Customers liked them better, so he did what was popular.)*
6. Is this good or bad? *(It is good if you are in business, for you must please your customers. If he had insisted on doing art nouveau windows when they were not popular, he would have made fewer windows; and since many were destroyed, we would not have many Tiffany windows left today. On the other hand, if he had done more of the truly best windows, we might have more truly great stained-glass works.)*
7. Look at the pictures of early cars. What did people call these early cars? What do they look like? *(horseless carriages; buggies that were pulled by horses)*
8. Automobile design is one of the first areas in which we see the result of industrial design for manufactured items. Which of these cars looks more like a machine than a wagon or buggy? *(the 1935 Lincoln Zephr)*
9. Which of these cars do you think was more aesthetically pleasing? *(Student answers will vary.)*
10. Which was better functionally? Why? *(The latter design is more functional. It looks heavier, more machinelike, more aerodynamic, and more like something designed to move speedily.)*
11. Name objects you have at home that were designed by an industrial designer. *(Student answers will vary widely but may include anything from small appliances to cars and tools.)*
12. Is industrial design important to your lifestyle? Why or why not? *(Yes. It makes things look nicer and makes them easier to use and clean.)*

Creative Expression Lessons

Lesson one: Paper stained-glass window

Materials needed
- newsprint, 18" × 24"
- rulers
- pencils
- colored pastels or crayons
- black, broad-tipped water-based markers
- black poster paper, 18" × 24"
- white chalkboard chalk
- pointed scissors or craft knives
- black plastic tape or transparent tape
- tissue paper (assorted colors)

- spray bottle
- cellophane (colored)
- small inexpensive paintbrushes
- white glue diluted half and half with water
- waxed paper or plastic bags to protect desks
- electric iron

Objective

The students will do the following:

- Plan a stained-glass design using black poster paper and transparent and translucent papers

Procedure (pp. 178-79)

1. On a piece of newsprint paper, lay out a stained-glass window design. Draw a half-inch frame all around the edges of the paper and then draw shapes. Avoid putting too much detail in the design (so that tiny pieces must be included) or using overly large sections of one color. Shapes must all touch each other and the frame.

2. Use colored pastels or crayons to plan the colors of your design. Remember to use flat colors and repeat them in several places. Go over your design with a water-based marker with a broad tip to make "lead lines."

3. Transfer the design to black poster paper with chalk. Trace both edges of your black outline.

4. Using pointed scissors or craft knives, cut out the spaces, allowing at least a one-eighth-inch width for the "lead lines." If the paper tears, repair it on the back side with black plastic tape or transparent tape.

5. Experiment with new colors and patterns by misting tissue paper with water from a spray bottle. Several colors laid together and misted will produce interesting color patterns like Tiffany's stained glass. You can wrinkle or fold the tissue paper and dip parts of it in water to produce patterned effects.

6. Turn the "leading" face down on the table and begin cutting pieces of tissue paper or cellophane to fit the spaces. The tissue paper or cellophane must be a little bigger than the opening to fit. Dampen a small paintbrush with diluted white glue and brush it on the back of the black paper; then stick the colored pieces into it. Do not use excess glue, or it will show. Protect your desk with waxed paper or plastic cleaner bags.

Caution: Do not let the diluted glue dry in the brush. Wash brushes immediately.

7. When all the colored papers have been glued on and dried, cut a piece of waxed paper to fit the back of the design and iron it on with a warm iron.

8. Display the designs in the windows for a colorful stained-glass effect. This is an effective way to decorate windows for Christmas or Easter season.

Assessment

- Evaluate student designs for craftsmanship, repeated color, and variety of shapes.

Lesson two: Faux batik stained glass

Materials needed

- newsprint
- pencils
- black, broad-tipped water-based markers
- tape
- unbleached muslin, washed in hot water to remove the sizing
- black permanent markers
- corrugated cardboard with a hole cut in the middle (The hole should be a little smaller than the cloth.)
- thumbtacks or masking tape
- wax crayons
- old electric skillet and small containers or a muffin tin, baking pan, and an electric hot plate
- inexpensive bristle brushes, not soft (These are for craft use and are made of hog bristle.)
- black dye (one package for two yards of fabric)
- large bucket or basin (stainless steel or enamel, not iron or aluminum)
- rubber or plastic gloves
- sink
- old newspapers (not new, or the ink may come off on the artwork)
- old electric iron
- sewing thread and needles
- dowel rods

Objective

The students will do the following:

- Plan and execute a stained-glass design, paint colors with melted crayon wax, and dye the finished cloth in black dye

Procedure (pp. 179-80)

1. Plan a design as in the previous lesson on newsprint paper. Your drawing can be a little freer on this design since shapes do not have to be cut out. Use several shapes and make sure every shape touches another shape or the border.

2. Trace over the design with a black marker. Tape a piece of unbleached muslin over the cartoon you have made and trace off the lines on the muslin with a black permanent marker. Stretch the muslin on a cardboard frame with thumbtacks or masking tape.

3. Melt wax crayons in small containers in an electric skillet with water in it. You can also use a muffin tin in a baking pan with water in it over a hot plate. Make sure there is always water in the skillet. The water will prevent the temperature from rising too high and starting a fire.

4. Using inexpensive bristle brushes, paint the melted wax onto the shapes in the batik; do not paint wax onto the black lines. If the wax is hot enough, it will completely penetrate the fabric; if it is too cool, the

wax will harden on top of the cloth and the design will not show when it is finished. Turn the fabric over frequently to check how well the wax is penetrating. If it is not penetrating well, paint the same color on the reverse side.

5. When all the shapes have been waxed, the fabric is ready for dyeing. Either crumple the fabric to make cracks in the wax or leave it flat. The direction and number of cracks can be controlled and planned to enhance the design. Mix the dye according to package directions in a large bucket or tub. If cold water dyes are available, use them; if not, allow the dye to cool before adding the fabric. Place the waxed fabric in the dye bath. Allow it to soak overnight until the color is darker than you want it. Remove the fabric and rinse it gently in cold water. Do not spray water directly onto it, or too much of the dye will rinse out, leaving a disappointing gray. Spread the fabric out in a cool place to dry—not in the sun.

6. When the fabric is dry, use old newspapers and an old iron to iron out the wax. It will take several layers of newspaper and much ironing to remove a good amount of the wax. You will never get it out entirely, so the fabric will remain stiff. Dry cleaning can remove the wax, but it may also dull the colors.

7. You can display your batik by fringing the edges of the fabric, making a casing or fabric loops, and hanging it from a dowel rod.

8. Make several batiks, starting with small sizes and working up to larger ones as you learn the technique. Evaluate your batiks for variety of shapes and sizes, repetition of colors, effective use of the black lines to unify and define the design, and division of the background into shapes. Then write a critique sheet on your best batik and turn it in to be graded.

Assessments
- Read the students' evaluation of their best work.
- Evaluate the work for repetition of color, effective use of shapes, and unity of design.

Lesson three: Stained-glass pendant

Materials needed
- stained-glass scraps
- black, fine-point permanent markers
- glass cutters
- safety goggles (even for students who wear glasses)
- chunks of broken glass, pebbles, and seashells (optional)
- copper foil for stained glass
- scissors
- fine steel wool
- old wood, flat stone, or ceramic tile
- flux and solder (Buy these at the same store and explain to a store employee what you are doing so that he can help you.)
- electric soldering gun with broad tip
- ring or pin back
- powdered sink cleanser
- old toothbrushes or small bristle brushes
- tissues
- dish detergent

Objectives
The students will do the following:
- Choose among scraps of stained glass and cut and file glass shapes to fit together
- Wrap glass pieces with copper foil and solder them together

Procedure (pp. 180-81)
1. Your teacher will have assembled from a local glass worker or hobby shop a box of glass scraps with a variety of colors and patterns. You may choose two to four pieces of glass to use in a pendant or pin. Even very small scraps can be used.

2. Use a fine-point permanent marker to draw shapes on the glass. Your teacher will demonstrate how to use a glass cutter to score the glass along the lines. Wear safety goggles when working with the glass. Avoid running the glass cutter over the same score two or three times; that dulls the cutter and makes it unusable. Tap the scored line with the ball on the end of the cutter until the glass breaks along the line. It may be necessary to file points off the edges of the glass. Do this with the teeth at the end of the cutter. Use the teeth to grind small chips off and smooth the edges. Lay the pieces together to test their fit. Make them fit as closely as possible; the more the edges touch, the stronger the product will be. Chunks of broken glass, pebbles, and seashells can be added if the glass pieces fit closely around them.

3. When all pieces have been shaped to fit closely together, wrap the edges with copper foil, folding it around on the front and back sides of the glass. Cut the foil so that it overlaps slightly at the ends. When all pieces have been foiled, clean them with fine steel wool and lay them together. Work on an old piece of wood or a flat piece of stone or ceramic tile. Apply flux to the corner where the pieces join and tack them with solder. Use a soldering iron with a broad tip on medium heat. Place the tip on the foil surface to heat it; then touch the solder to the surface to melt it. Once it melts and runs, remove the iron immediately. Tack each corner the same way. Using the same process, run a line of solder along all the edges, covering the foil completely and making a smooth line. Keep the gun moving: if you pause too long, you may melt the solder completely off the foil.

4. Solder on a ring or other materials such as pin backs. To clean the pendant, lay it flat on the table and sprinkle it with powdered sink cleanser. Use a small bristle brush, like an old toothbrush, to scrub first one side then the other. Rinse off the cleanser and let it dry. When the work has dried, a fine powder may show; polish this off with a tissue and wash the pendant in warm soapy water. Let it dry again.

Problems: If solder runs through onto the work surface, the soldering iron is too hot or you are keeping it on the work too long. Be sure you have the right kind of flux for the solder you are using. Once you have cleaned the foiled pieces, do not touch them with your hands. Keep your hands clean: greasy fingerprints keep solder from sticking. If glass and other pieces do not touch on the edges, you will have difficulty soldering them. Be careful as you cut and shape the pieces to avoid gaps. Wrap copper foil carefully and smoothly around the edges of the glass.

Assessments
- Demonstrate and assist students in cutting and filing glass shapes.
- Evaluate students' work for pleasing color choices and good craftsmanship.

Chapter 15: Rouault, to the Glory of God

Seeing and Perceiving (pp. 187-89)

Questions and Answers

Head of Christ

1. What event in Christ's life is portrayed in this painting? *(The event portrayed is Christ's suffering—His beating—before the Crucifixion.)*

2. Does the painting make you think of any Bible verses? Find as many verses as you can about this event and read them. *(Psalm 22:6-8; Isaiah 53:2-7; Matthew 27:27-31; Mark 15:16-20; John 19:1-5)*

3. How did Rouault create an emotional effect? *(He used dark, slashing lines and cool colors.)* What effect does this picture have on you? *(Answers will vary; most will probably respond with descriptive words like* ugly, revolting, pitiable, *or* scary.*)* Why do these methods create such a strong emotional effect? *(The lines look as though they are cutting up the face; we associate the colors with bruises and wounds.)*

4. What effect does this style have on the three-dimensional structure of the figure? *(It flattens it; the painting has neither mass nor space.)*

5. Does the painting look as though it was done quickly or slowly? *(Most students will probably guess that it was done quickly. Actually, Rouault painted many of his works slowly and patiently, examining each stage before adding to it.)*

6. Look especially at the eyes. What do they express? *(They are full of suffering and fatigue, looking up to heaven, fully conscious.)*

7. Why do you think he focused so closely on the head? *(He did so to force us to see what Christ went through, to focus on the suffering, and to remove the temptation to see just a good picture.)*

Understanding and Evaluating (pp. 189-90)

Questions and Answers

1. Would you call this painting realistic? *(probably not, since realism is usually defined)*

2. What similarities are there between this painting and a caricature? *(It resembles the subject but is also changed; it exaggerates facial features and expressions; it focuses on the face.)*

3. What differences are there? *(A caricature usually pokes fun at a person's dominant features: big nose, wrinkles, hairstyle, large ears, and so forth; this painting seems much more serious in effect.)*

4. Let's imagine you have no idea who this person was: you have never heard of Christianity and know nothing about the story. What would you know by looking at this painting? *(The person has been beaten; he is not rebelling or fighting; he is looking up at something as though he hoped for help; he is not angry; something unjust is happening.)*

5. In what sense did Rouault confound art and life? *(His pictures are always about what happens in real life; they symbolize problems dealt with in real life.)*

6. Did any other artists before Rouault confound art and life? *(Most of them did, though not always as strongly or as negatively; protest artists such as Goya and Daumier were especially noted for this characteristic.)*

7. If the artist does not mix art and life, what will he have to express? *(Students' answers will vary. Point out, however, that such an artist will express feelings about color, line, shape, and so on; his expression will be art about art instead of art about life.)*

8. Does this help you see where modern nonobjectivism originated? *(When artists stopped making art about what happened in real life, they started making pictures that were nonobjective.)*

9. Until later in Rouault's life, his art was not much appreciated by either the French government, the museums, or the Catholic Church. Why do you think this was so? *(It was too strong, not pretty enough, and told the truth too harshly.)*

10. Do you remember what his teacher, Gustave Moreau, told him about popularity? *(He told him to be glad that he did not have popularity right away; it would give him time to reveal himself fully without pressure.)* Do you think he was right? *(Students' answers will vary; however, opinions should be supported by sound reasoning.)*

11. Is it a good idea for governments, museums, and churches to embrace every new concept that appears in art? *(There are two possible points of view here: no, it is better to wait to see what turns out to be truly good; yes, otherwise the artist suffers too much. Encourage students to support their viewpoint.)*

12. Will the lack of sales and popularity stop a true artist from creating? *(No, if he really wants to create, he will do whatever it takes to live and still create.)*

Creative Expression Lessons

Lesson one: Gesture drawing

Materials needed

- newsprint, 18" × 24"
- drawing board, larger than 18" × 24"
- masking tape
- black wax crayons or design ebony pencils

Objective

The students will do the following:

- Use freely drawn lines that describe gesture rather than form

Procedure (p. 190)

1. One student at a time will model for the rest of the class. The model may stand or sit but should be in a position that implies movement: leaning, turning, legs crossed, or reaching. The pose will need to be held for two or three minutes.
2. Tape a piece of newsprint paper to a drawing board.
3. Study the pose to determine the major lines that describe the movement the figure is making. You will probably begin with the back and add the limbs later. Do not draw the shape; use the lines to show the movement and balance.
4. Add freely drawn circular shapes to indicate the weight of the body, but do not draw specific shapes or details since these are short two- to three-minute sketches.
5. After all members of the class have had a chance to pose for a drawing, your teacher will conduct a class critique so that you can see how others used lines to express movement.

Assessments

- Observe students and guide any who are having difficulty. Encourage them to make loose, free lines that do not show details.
- Have class members pick out the most effective designs.

Lesson two: Painting with free line and color

Materials needed

- still-life objects, including a chair or stool
- model with costume
- sheets of gray bogus paper
- tempera paint (variety of colors)
- watercolor brushes, size 10-12
- egg cartons or small jars

Objective

The students will do the following:

- Draw and paint life-size objects on large sheets of bogus paper.

Procedure (pp. 190-91)

1. Your teacher will instruct some of you to bring in interesting objects such as large potted plants, patterned wallpaper, patterned fabric or cushions, a small lamp, and so forth. The arrangement should have some vertical and some horizontal elements, several patterns, lots of color, overlapping items, and interesting views from all sides.
2. Someone will model for the class, perhaps wearing a costume related to a specific activity (such as a formal dress or suit, work clothes, or a foreign costume). The model will sit on a stool or chair and be surrounded by the objects.
3. The still life with the model will be too large even for large pieces of paper, so plan what parts of the arrangement to use. Keep the center of interest somewhere near but not exactly at the center of the paper. Use lines and shapes of the objects to point to the center of interest. Eliminate or reposition objects that would be confusing to the viewer.
4. Draw the major lines with black or dark-colored tempera paint, thinned with water to flow easily. Draw the same way you practiced the gesture drawings. Do not include too many details. Hang up the drawings to see if all the important objects are included and whether you can tell what they are. Drawings can be reworked because the colors will cover the lines you do not want.
5. Decide whether you will use a color scheme of mostly bright, warm colors or mostly cool, neutral colors. Mix colors in advance and keep them in an old egg carton or small jars. Mix enough to finish the painting without running out. Colors do not need to be local colors; you may vary them in order to follow your color scheme. Small areas of contrast colors may be used, but most of the colors should follow the color scheme. Paint colors loosely into the spaces between the lines. Cover unwanted lines with thick paint but do not brush over them a second time; otherwise, the dark paint will mix into the color and dull it. Objects can be shaded with several values of color, but most of the painting will be rather flat.

Assessment

- Evaluate the finished paintings for center of interest, freely drawn lines, and use of a color scheme.

Lesson three: Expressive drawing of a figure

Materials needed

- model in worn work clothes
- tools, tool belt
- newsprint
- soft drawing pencils, 2B-3B
- white drawing paper, 18" × 24"
- colored pencils (optional)

Objectives

The students will do the following:

The Modern World

- Draw a model according to the mood, emotion, or experience they want to express
- Draw a longer study of the model and add necessary details and small amounts of color or shading

Procedure (pp. 191-92)

1. Your teacher will choose a young man from outside the class to model. He will wear worn work clothes and will have a tool belt, tools, or other small equipment. Your class will discuss the model's occupation based on the tools used and determine what he is experiencing: hunger, fatigue, heat, strength, pride, and so forth. Choose what mood you want to give the picture. Your teacher will choose a pose for the model based on all the students' suggestions.

2. Start with a few small gesture drawings of the model, trying to capture the movement and pose.

3. With a large sheet of drawing paper, plan your drawing so that you have room enough to draw all of the model on the paper. Draw a longer study of the pose, using freely drawn lines. As you draw, you may add a few details and tighten up the drawing a little, but remember that what is important is to communicate how the subject feels and what he is experiencing, not how he looks.

4. Add just enough details to help the viewer understand what the subject is doing—nothing extra.

5. You may wish to add a small amount of color or shading to the drawing, but do not fill in all the spaces. The color may help you to express the mood better. It should not be important for its own sake, though.

Assessment

- Evaluate the finished drawings for their use of convincing movement, expression of what the model was experiencing, and effective use of color or shading.

Chapter 16: *Feeling for Humanity, Kollwitz and Barlach*

The Historical Background (pp. 198-99)

Suggestion: Erich Remarque's *All Quiet on the Western Front* effectively evokes the horror of World War I. You may wish to read portions of the book to your eleventh and twelfth grade students to help give them a feel for the war and how it affected Europeans.

Note: You may find a copy of Dali's famous *Persistence of Memory* in many art appreciation or art history textbooks.

Seeing and Perceiving (pp. 199-201)

Questions and Answers

In God's Hands

1. Can you see the marks on the surface that look like clay that has been modeled by something? Do you think Kollwitz used a tool, or did she use her fingers? Why do you think so? (*The shapes are all rather soft or rounded. They do not look as though they were cut with a tool. The sleeve at the right appears to have fingerprints on it.*)

2. What do you see in the sculpture? (*a face, three hands, and a sleeve or robe of some kind*)

3. Whose face do you think it is? (*Answers will vary. It could possibly be the face of the artist or her son who had been killed or just a general face that could be anybody's.*)

4. What does the expression on the face tell you? (*The expression looks calm and peaceful; maybe the person had died; maybe the person is just resting.*)

5. Does the expression symbolize anything? (*Answers will vary; it could symbolize faith, confidence, or fear.*)

6. Notice the size of the hands. Why are they so different? (*God's hands are bigger to symbolize His strength.*)

7. Look at what the hands are doing. Describe the actions. (*The smaller hand is grasping the cloak tightly as though he is afraid to let go; God's hands are relaxed. He is supporting and holding onto the person gently, protectingly.*)

8. This sculpture is a metaphor. Do you remember what a metaphor is in literature? The artist has given us the meaning in the title *In God's Hands*. What is the earthly picture she uses to show that relationship? (*She uses the picture of a father protecting a child from some fear or danger.*)

9. Notice how one form seems to melt into the other so that all of it looks inseparable. Does that help reinforce the subject? How? (*It reinforces it by increasing the impression of security; no one can separate the small figure from the larger one, so it is protected.*)

10. Why do you think Kollwitz did not show God's face? (*Maybe she felt it would be idolatry; it was not really necessary—the hands say it all; a face would have distracted us from the hands; it is God's hand that He refers to when He describes Himself as the protector of His Old Testament people. See Exodus 3:20; 15:6 and Deuteronomy 3:24.*)

11. Do you think her opinion of God had changed by the time she did this sculpture? (*It seems as though she does not see Him as remote anymore.*)

The Avenger

12. What is *The Avenger* doing? (*running, chasing someone*) How fast does he seem to be moving? (*He is moving so fast that he looks as though he may lose his balance; he looks almost as though he is flying.*)

13. He did not sculpt nude figures. Instead, his figures are revealed by the draping of the cloth. In *The Avenger*, what does the garment show us about the body? (*It shows where his feet and legs are; it shows the arm reaching; it shows the speed of his movement.*)

14. The body is hidden by the garment, and many sculptors disliked Barlach's sculpture for that reason. But he wants to focus on something other than the body. What do you think it is? (*He wants to focus on the emotional intensity; The Avenger is determined, single-minded, dedicated; everything is given over to reckless pursuit of his goal; the lines of the robe steer us to the head where the intensity is focused.*)

15. What is the figure pursuing and why? (*You cannot tell, since there is no hint; some students may speculate, but point out to them that there is no indication in the sculpture itself.*) Why do you suppose Hitler disliked this sculpture? (*Answers will vary. However, students should note that Hitler's desire to reduce art to a vehicle for political statement would in itself have made this work unacceptable. As the title—The Avenger—suggests, Barlach's work deals with a universal truth rather than a temporal concept. It does not explicitly state that the "avenger" is out to right the wrongs of Hitler's Germany, but neither does it explicitly praise the regime's "moral code." It is this very ambiguity that would have angered Hitler and awakened in him the paranoia characteristic of a corrupt mind.*)

16. How is this different from narrative sculpture? (*It does not tell a story as history painting does; there is no detail to it.*)

Understanding and Evaluating (pp. 201-2)

Questions and Answers

1. Perhaps the sculpture is symbolic. If so, what might it symbolize? *(It might symbolize war, one nation taking vengeance on another; an individual in the war getting vengeance for a dead soldier; God taking vengeance on a nation for its evil.)*

2. Barlach wanted his figures to suggest more than just the earthly: he wanted them to suggest the soul. "Where does man come from? Certainly not the ape," says Barlach. "I do not think of myself as descending from the past, . . . but from up front, from above." Do you think he succeeded in suggesting the soul of this figure? *(Students will have varying opinions, but they should be able to support their opinions.)*

3. Both of these artists used their art to expose the evils of their day. Do you think their work is weaker or stronger because of that? *(Students will have varying opinions, but they should be able to support their opinions.)*

4. Read I Peter 4:10; make a list of ways in which one could serve others in the church or community by using art. *(Students' answers will vary.)*

5. In what sense does Barlach use the word *relax*? *(He uses the word emotionally, meaning no inner tension, no stress; he certainly does not mean physical relaxation.)*

6. Compare this definition with the works of these artists. How are these works like propaganda art? How are they different? *(Their works both express issues that are specific and could be taken to be partisan. Their issues are not really temporary; they deal with events that have always happened to people. They avoid details that identify their characters with a specific event; they both find creative ways to express their concerns without telling a narrative.)*

Creative Expression Lessons

Lesson one: Proportional study

Materials needed
- white drawing paper, 9" × 12"
- pencils
- window
- rulers
- magazine photos of a face or photocopies of a picture of a face

Objectives
The students will do the following:
- Diagram the proportions of the human face
- Compare generic proportions with magazine or newspaper photos or snapshots

Procedure (pp. 202-3)

1. Fold a 9" × 12" piece of drawing paper in half the long way exactly down the middle. Draw half of a large egg shape (large enough to make a mask) on one half of the paper with its center on the fold. An egg has one end that is round; the other end is slightly pointed. A human head has a somewhat similar shape.

2. Put the folded paper on a windowpane so that the sun shines through it and trace the shape onto the other side of the paper. Open the paper flat and you should have the outline of the head. The head should not be round, nor should it be too narrow. Incorrect proportions will distort the facial features, although distorted features might make a humorous mask.

3. Measure halfway from the top of the head to the bottom and mark that spot on the face. Then measure one quarter from the top and three quarters from the top to the bottom and mark those spots.

4. On the halfway mark, measure across the face horizontally and mark off five equal spaces. These will be used to space the eyes. Since each eye takes up one-fifth of the width of the face, draw the eyes one space wide and with one space between them for the bridge of the nose. On the one-quarter mark above the eyes place the hairline; on the three-quarter mark place the bottom of the nose. Halfway between the bottom of the nose and the chin, place the mouth. Slightly above the eyes, draw the eyebrows. In an adult, the ears begin at the level of the eyebrows and end near the bottom of the nose.

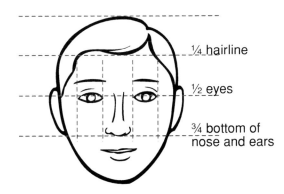

5. Refine the drawing of the features, making it neater and adding details like eyelids, lips, and shading.

6. Find a large picture of a face in a magazine or newspaper, or use a snapshot from home and enlarge it on a copier. Compare your proportional chart to the proportions of the face in the photo. Draw the lines on the magazine picture or copy you made. Are they the same or different? List the differences.

Assessments
- Evaluate the students' diagrams to see if they followed directions and used reasonably good proportion.

- Compare the students' diagrams to the measurements they made on the photographs and evaluate the differences they found.

Lesson two: Relief face

Materials needed
- heavy-weight polyethylene (16" × 20" mats)
- nonhardening oil-based modeling clay
- pencils or modeling tools
- paper towels
- old shirt or apron to protect clothes
- mirror (optional)

Objective
The students will do the following:
- Make a relief face with naturalistic structure and proportion. They will decide whether to give it a facial expression and what expression to use

Procedure (p. 203)
1. You will be working on a plastic mat with about half a pound of oil-based modeling clay.
2. Work the clay with your hands until it warms up and becomes pliable. Then form an oval shape that is mounded up on the plastic. Remember the shape of the head in your diagram from Lesson one.
3. By pinching, pressing, or adding bits of clay, begin to hollow out the eye area and raise the nose. As you model, study your face in the mirror and feel it with your hands to identify raised and lowered areas. Keep paper towels nearby to wipe your hands on so that clay does not get on your face and clothes. It is an oil-based clay that will wash off, but it will leave grease stains.
4. Use the diagram from Lesson one to evaluate the proportion and position of each of the features. Include such important structures as eyelids, cheek bones, the ridge of the nose and eyebrows, and the lips and chin.
5. If you wish to give your relief a facial expression, look at your own facial expressions in the mirror to guide you. Avoid extreme expressions.
6. Finish the relief by adding hair, a hat, a neck and collar, and so forth. Smooth the surface of the clay with your fingers or leave it rough.

Note: If oil-based clay is used, the sculpture cannot be kept—the clay will be reused. If self-hardening clay is used, students may keep their sculptures.

Assessment
- Evaluate each student's relief, looking for facial structure, proportion, and expression.

Lesson three: Plaster casting

Materials needed
- cardboard boxes, a little larger and deeper than the clay reliefs
- plastic sheets and clay reliefs from Lesson two
- vegetable oil
- brushes
- plaster of Paris (When mixing plaster of Paris, add powder to water until both are at the same level. Do not whip bubbles into it. Mix gently.)
- plastic bowls for mixing plaster
- water
- shellac
- paper clips
- furniture polish or neutral shoe polish
- brown shoe polish or thinned acrylic paint (to color sculpture)
- black shoe polish (to antique a colored sculpture)

Note: Each student will need a shallow cardboard box a little larger than the relief he made in Lesson two. Place the plastic sheet with the clay relief on it in the bottom of the box, facing up. The sides of the box need to be higher than the highest part of the relief.

Objective
The students will do the following:
- Make a mold from their clay relief and cast a plaster model

Procedure (p. 204)
1. Using the box supplied by your teacher, place the plastic sheet with the clay relief on it in the bottom of the box, facing up.
2. Paint the clay and the plastic sheeting with vegetable oil, coating it completely.
3. Mix up a small container of plaster of Paris according to the directions on the package. When it is an even consistency without lumps, slowly pour it over the relief sculpture, allowing it to fill in all the spaces around the sides. Shake the box gently to drive out air bubbles.
4. Set it aside overnight till it is firm to the touch. Carefully remove the box and clay form and let the plaster dry to the touch.
5. Lay the plaster mold on the table and paint it with shellac. When the shellac has dried, paint it with vegetable oil to keep the sculpture medium from sticking to the mold. Put the mold back into the box.
6. Mix and pour more plaster of Paris into the mold; bury half of a paper clip in the plaster at the top to serve as a hanger. Let it harden. Carefully remove it and let it air dry.
7. Wax it with furniture polish and buff it to give it a shiny surface, or use shoe polish to color and shine it. Plaster can also be painted with thinned acrylic paint to make it look like bronze. Antiquing it with black shoe polish accentuates the relief.

Assessment

- Evaluate the castings by comparing them with the original reliefs and examining the patina and its appropriateness to the face.

Lesson four: Wood carving

Materials needed

- white pine or other soft wood (a two-by-four board cut into 10"-12" blocks)
- wood carving knives
- white paper
- pencils
- clear shoe polish or wood stain and brown shoe polish
- wooden base
- carpenter's glue or screw, screwdriver, and drill

Objective

The students will do the following:

- Draw a figure on all sides of the block of wood and carve the figure

Procedure (pp. 204-5)

1. Your teacher will supply you with a carving knife and a ten- to twelve-inch block of white pine cut from a two-by-four board.

2. Draw the outline of your block on a piece of white paper. Plan the figure so that it touches the edges of the block in several places. Make the figure compact: keep the arms against the body and do not allow small parts to protrude. Draw it from all sides.

3. Transfer these drawings to the block of wood on all four sides. Make sure the front and back line up with each other.

4. Visualize the figure "imprisoned" inside the block, as Michelangelo would have said. All you have to do is carve away everything that is not your figure—simple, right?

5. Start on the corners, carving away until you get close to the form. You will have to carve away your drawing in some places. Keep turning your carving around as you work. Always carve with the grain, not across it. Do not carve toward your hand; keep your hands under the sculpture or behind the knife. Keep the knives sharp—nothing is more dangerous than a dull knife.

6. As you work, keep revisualizing the figure and carving in toward it. Be careful not to remove too much wood.

7. Remove as many rough spots as possible with the carving knife, but knife marks should show.

8. When the figure is finished, you can wax it with clear shoe polish to preserve the light color of the wood, or stain it with wood stain and polish it with brown shoe polish to bring out the textures.

9. Make a base out of a separate square of wood, and glue or screw your figure to it.

Assessments

- Help the class organize a sculpture exhibition in the classroom or the hallway of the school. Have the students choose the best view of each sculpture and display it in that position.
- Evaluate each sculpture for its pose and reasonably good technique of carving.

Chapter 17: The Cult of Imagination, Salvador Dali

Seeing and Perceiving (p. 211)

Questions and Answers

The Sacrament of the Last Supper

1. One of the typical effects Dali used is a sort of visual multiplication—he sometimes repeats a figure, though with modifications. Compare the right and left halves of the painting. Do you see any repeated figures? *(The disciples are exact repetitions of each other with different colors used.)*

2. What is in the empty space in front of the mountains? How do you know? *(It is a large lake; there are reflections in the water.)*

3. What did most of these men do for a living before they met Jesus? How does Dali show that? *(They were fishermen; Dali puts at least one empty boat in the water near the foreground.)*

4. Where are Christ and the disciples in relation to the landscape? *(They are in front of it, in the foreground.)*

5. Are they indoors or outdoors? Why do you think so? *(Students may have several explanations. Following are three possible answers: (1) They are indoors; the space looks enclosed, and it seems to be lit from the large window behind Christ; (2) They are outdoors; the bars of the window and the wall dissolve so that you can see the mountains through them, and the shadows are too dark to be indoors. (3) It is ambiguous; indoors and outdoors flow together without clear distinction.)*

6. Is their space continuous with the background—could you walk from where they are to the lake? *(No, they appear to be up high—in a building looking down on the lake but separated from it.)*

7. If the light is coming from the large window behind Christ, why is the table in front of Him so light? *(He seems transparent; perhaps the light is shining through Him.)*

8. Why are there two straight streaks of light on the ends of the table? Why aren't the shadows shaped like the men? *(These elements seem completely arbitrary—not related to anything in the scene—yet they do make it look as if light is shining into the room.)*

Understanding and Evaluating (pp. 212-13)

Questions and Answers

1. What are the two adjectives he uses to describe "instantaneousness"? *(Pythagorean and luminous)*

2. Look up Pythagoreanism in the dictionary. What does it mean? *(the description of reality in mathematical terms)* Later, we will understand the role math plays in this work.

3. What does luminous mean? How does this fit with the painting? *(full of light or emitting light; the painting is filled with light; the light might even appear to be shining from the sky)*

4. Dali sometimes symbolized purity by using the device of levitation. Does that help explain the figure of Jesus in the top of this painting? *(yes)*

5. Look at Christ's gestures. What do you think He is saying to the disciples? *(He seems to be gesturing to Himself with one hand and pointing upward with the other, perhaps saying, "I am the way" or "I will drink no more of the fruit of the vine, until that day that I drink it new in the kingdom of God.")*

6. What are the disciples doing? *(They seem to be worshiping; they are not looking at Christ. Perhaps they are saddened by what they hear.)*

7. Does this picture represent a literal illustration of the event in the Bible? *(no)*

8. Can you identify any of the disciples? *(probably not)* Which one is Judas? *(We cannot tell.)*

9. If the painting does not illustrate what happened, what does it show? *(Maybe it shows a sacrament or memorial service in which the participants imagine that Jesus is there. Maybe it pictures what the disciples believe instead of what they see.)*

10. The Catholic Church has a doctrine called transubstantiation. Remembering that Dali was a very loyal Catholic, can you see how this painting fits in with the Catholic view of the Lord's Supper? *(Christ is transparent in both places; He is in essence with them even though the bread and wine are all we see.)*

11. The architectural structure that looks like an odd-shaped window behind Christ is part of a dodecahedron. Greek mathematicians used the dodecahedron as a symbol for the universe. Dali was also thinking of the significance of the number twelve. How many objects that come in sets of twelve can you think of? *(Students' answers will vary; following are some possibilities: twelve hours on the clock; twelve months in the year; twelve sides on the dodecahedron; twelve apostles; twelve tribes of Israel.)*

12. Why do you think Dali used a dodecahedron in this painting? *(He did so to show that Christ was universal or Creator of the universe, that He is ruler of the universe, and that the universe is His home.)*

13. Some critics have said that the Christian paintings of Dali seem technically perfect but emotionally cool. Do you agree or disagree? Why? *(Students' answers will vary. Encourage them to explain their viewpoints.)*

14. Can you think of some secular attitudes today that are related to surrealist attitudes? *(Many people think of the church as irrelevant; they identify and blame God for what churches and Christians do; people value emotions rather than logic; people think the way to solve problems is to rebel against authorities; they sometimes assume that imagination is irrational.)*

Creative Expression Lessons

Lesson one: Mathematical analysis

Materials needed
- a photocopy of the *The Sacrament of the Last Supper* for each student (You may prefer to enlarge the copies. If you wish to reuse the copies, laminate them first.)
- tracing paper as large as the photocopy
- colored pencils or pens or projector markers
- overhead projector (if needed)
- rulers

Objective
The students will do the following:
- Draw a grid showing the golden section and compare the mathematical grid to the painting

Procedure (pp. 213-14)
1. Lay a sheet of tracing paper over the reproduction of Dali's *Sacrament of the Last Supper.* Trace the outside edges of the painting onto your tracing paper.

2. Remove the tracing paper from the painting and place it on a plain surface.

3. To find the golden rectangle, measure one of the shorter sides of the outline and, along the top and bottom edges, mark off that distance from the right and left sides. Draw a vertical line from top to bottom at those measurements.

4. Now divide the painting exactly in half in both directions—horizontally and vertically—and draw those lines across it.

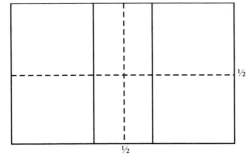

5. Now place the diagram you have drawn over the copy of the painting. Notice where the lines fall in rela-

tion to the objects and people in the painting. What relationships do you observe? *(Jesus is on the center line; the middle horizontal line is the horizon line; this line cuts through His mouth. The two "golden section" lines cut through the men to His left and right; other than these two men, Jesus is alone in the center space.)*

6. Look for other mathematical relationships in the painting. *(If you divide the painting into equal quarters from side to side, the one-quarter and three-quarter lines pass through the men in front of the table; the distance from the horizon line to the front of the table is exactly the same as the distance from the top of the painting to the horizontal of the dodecahedron; the arms of the ascending Christ are parallel to the streaks of light on the table; the arms of the ascending Christ can also be seen as the arc of a large circle that is like an umbrella over all the disciples.)*

7. Dali has used one of the same devices that Leonardo da Vinci used five hundred years ago to portray Christ. On the tracing paper, draw a line from Christ's head down to a piece of bread on the table, then across to the other piece and up to His head again. What geometric shape do you find? *(an equilateral triangle)* Leonardo used the exact same shape in his painting of the Last Supper. Why do you suppose both artists chose this shape? *(to symbolize the Trinity; because it is an enduring shape like the pyramids; it calls attention to the center)*

8. Sometimes traditional artists used linear perspective to direct our eyes to some important point in the painting. Use a ruler to trace the lines at the sides of the table and the shadows to their vanishing point. Where is it? *(almost exactly on His mouth)*

9. Now find the two diagonal lines of the dodecahedron that frame the ascending Christ. Trace their lines with the ruler. Where do they point? *(to the bread on the opposite side; they make an X through the head of Christ)* Do you see any of the other lines of the dodecahedron that point to something else? *(The slanting lines of the bottom of the dodecahedron line up with the slant of the men in the foreground.)*

Assessments
- If necessary, you can demonstrate each step on an overhead projector to assist students in drawing and measuring.
- Listen as students explain what they have observed about the relation between the lines and the subjects in the painting.

Lesson two: Memory montage

Materials needed
- old magazines, books, photo albums for research
- pencils

- moderately heavyweight drawing paper, 60-80 lb., or Bristol board
- acrylic, tempera, or watercolor paints
- brushes
- glue sticks or paste
- matboard (optional)
- scissors
- rulers
- tracing paper
- double-sided transparent tape, reusable adhesive, or mounting putty

Objectives

The students will do the following:

- Draw and paint a background as illusionistically as possible
- Cut pictures of objects that have personal symbolism for them and paste them onto the painted background

Procedure (pp. 214-15)

1. In books, photographs, and magazines, search for a background for your montage. It might be a landscape, a seascape, a city, or an interior scene that reminds you of a place you associate with your past. Draw the scene on a piece of moderately heavyweight paper and paint it as illusionistically as you can. Colors can be changed or adjusted to fit the overall idea. If you do not have much time, find a large magazine picture for the background and paste it onto a piece of matboard.

2. Look through magazines for pictures of objects or people that remind you of experiences or dreams you have had. Use some objects as symbols. Cut carefully: be sure not to leave any background around the edge of the selected object so that the picture will blend into the montage.

3. With a ruler, a pencil, and a piece of tracing paper, try some mathematical schemes for organizing your composition. Try dividing the painting in halves or thirds or vertically. Try introducing diagonal or curved lines or geometric shapes. Draw these lines on the tracing paper. Lay the tracing paper over your background.

4. Lay the cutout objects you have collected on the tracing paper so that they correspond with lines of the composition and are also where you want them on the background. Use double-sided tape or reusable adhesive to hold them in place. One by one, paste the cutouts onto the painted background.

5. Explain your montage to the class.

Assessments

- Have each student explain his montage and his experience to the class.
- Evaluate the composition, technique, and expressive communication of the montages.

Lesson three: Animal visions

Materials needed

- Bibles
- stovepipe wire
- old newspaper
- shallow pan big enough to mix paste in
- wallpaper paste
- objects for texture (pebbles, leaves, string, wire, beads, seeds, etc.)
- acrylic paints
- brushes

Objectives

The students will do the following:

- Think of an animal combination or use one suggested by the Scripture passages given
- Build a sculpture with papier-mâché

Procedure (p. 215)

1. Think of two animals you would like to combine into one. Imagine an animal with a long neck and short legs or a thin, long-legged animal with an elephant's trunk. Or take an idea from one of the following Scripture passages: Daniel 4:32-35, Nebuchadnezzar's insanity; Daniel 7:1-8, Daniel's vision of the earth's kingdoms; Ezekiel 1:5-11, Ezekiel's vision of the cherubim; Revelation 13:1-3, the beast of the Tribulation.

2. Using stovepipe wire, make an armature about one foot tall for the main body parts of your animal. Fill the armature with crumpled, dry newspaper to build up the form of the creature. Pose the armature and make sure it stands solidly by itself.

3. Make a pan of wallpaper paste, mixing it till it is free of lumps and about the thickness of hot cereal. Make papier-mâché by dipping small strips of newspaper into the paste and applying them to the structure, covering the wire and crumpled newspaper. You can make little lumps of papier-mâché to build up the form. Be sure to smooth out the paper strips while they are wet so that the surface is smooth. Continue to add layers of papier-mâché to the sculpture. Let the paste dry overnight or longer in a warm, dry place. If the weather is humid, placing the sculpture in a warm oven will help it dry. Avoid pasting new layers of paper over layers that are still wet, or the entire sculpture may grow moldy. Create texture on the surface by gluing pebbles, leaves, string, wire, or other such objects to it.

4. When the form is complete and dry, paint the surface with acrylic paints. Include details such as scales, color variations, ears, horns, eyes, and so forth.

Assessment

- Evaluate sculptures on the creativity of their interpretation of the animal, logical structure, technique, texture, and color used.

The Modern World

Chapter 18: *Art to the Rescue, Barnett Newman*

Seeing and Perceiving (pp. 221-22)

Questions and Answers

Stations of the Cross

1. Look at the reproduction of the *First Station*. Why do you think Newman limited himself to so few colors? *(He did so to make it more stark, to emphasize sorrow and death, and to emphasize purity versus evil.)*

2. What other details can you see? *(a broad black strip down the left side, a lot of empty space, and two ragged stripes at the right)*

3. What elements are repeated to unify the picture? *(straight vertical lines on sides and on the black strip and the off-white zip; the colors black and off-white)*

4. What elements are varied to provide contrast? *(the smooth edges of the black area at left and the off-white zip versus the rough edges of the black area along the zip)*

5. Compare the *Twelfth Station* to the *First Station*. What other similarities do you notice? *(colors, straight and jagged lines, placement of the strip on the left and the zip on the right is the same in both)*

6. The painting is six feet six inches tall and five feet wide. How does this size relate to a person's size? *(It is about as large as a man with his arms stretched out.)* Tape off a rectangle on the wall the exact size of the painting with the bottom of the rectangle touching the floor. Your teacher will have a man who is at least six feet tall stand in front of the rectangle and reach his hands above his head and out to the sides at an angle. Do his hands reach the corners of the rectangle? How does this position relate to the *Stations of the Cross*? *(It is the position of a crucified man.)*

7. After looking at these paintings, do you understand why this style came to be called minimal? Is there more to look at than you thought at first glance? List items that are not included that would have been included in a seventeenth-century picture. *(figures, background, tools and props, textures, colors, facial expressions, sky and clouds, etc.)*

Understanding and Evaluating (pp. 223-26)

Questions and Answers

1. What is the subject matter of this series? *(The subject is the Crucifixion, the suffering of Christ, His death—all deaths.)*

2. Some of the characteristics that produce an experience of the sublime in art are darkness, silence, emptiness, and a large size. How do these relate to Barnett Newman's *Stations of the Cross*? *(the large size of his paintings, his use of black, leaving the middle of the canvas plain, use of bare canvas that seems empty)*

3. Look at the previous list of the stations of the cross to see the focus of the twelfth station. *(Christ's death)*

4. In the *Twelfth Station*, what does the amount of black suggest to you? *(death, unconsciousness, or pain)* With Christ's death in mind, how could you interpret the other elements in the painting? *(Students' answers will vary; however, make sure they have reasons related to the painting, not just speculations.)*

5. According to this interpretation, what would black stand for? *(consciousness, life, pain, or suffering)* What would off-white stand for? *(unconsciousness, death, eternity, or peace)*

6. Would these symbols work the same way in *First Station*? *(The black would work the same way; the off-white would work only as peace or tranquility, not unconsciousness, death, or eternity. Students will have other opinions; evaluate the reasoning behind what they say.)*

7. What other interpretation could you think of for the rough-edged zip at the right? *(The jagged edges could emphasize the brutality and ugliness of the event; they could also suggest the vulnerability of humanity, while their verticality suggests the upward striving of man; the off-white line may portray stabbing pain.)*

8. What relationships did you find? *(The black strip at the left is one-third of the area at the right; that area is one-third of the width from the left edge to the zip.)*

9. If you count up all the separate units that make up these three sections, how many parts is the canvas divided into? *(three plus nine—twelve)*

10. In the *Twelfth Station* the black area ends just after the zip that ends the ninth division of the picture. What does this suggest? Look at Matthew 27:46. *(It was the ninth hour when Jesus cried out and then died.)*

11. Divide into groups and read the excerpts of reviews you receive from your teacher. These were published about the international show *The New American Painting*, which traveled throughout Europe in 1958 and 1959. Newman was one of the artists featured. For each review, note whether the reviewer is favorable to the new art, unfavorable, or ambivalent. List the specific characteristics the reviewer likes or dislikes about the work on the chalkboard. Get a book that contains reproductions of several abstract expressionist works and compare the lists to reproductions of the

paintings. Try to understand why the reviewer said what he said. With which reviews do you agree or disagree? Why? *(Students' answers will vary; however, encourage them to explain their viewpoints.)*

Note: See Appendix page 70 for reviews.

Creative Expression Lessons

Lesson one: Designing a radial

Materials needed
- white drawing paper, 9" × 12"
- rulers
- compasses
- triangles
- pencils
- white vinyl erasers
- colored pencils
- scissors
- paper glue
- colored or black construction paper trimmed to 12" squares

Objectives
The students will do the following:
- Create a radial design (starting with a grid) with a variety of shapes
- Color the shapes, preserving the radial quality

Procedure (p. 227)
1. Choose whether to use a circle or square as the basis for your design.
2. Draw the circle or square using a ruler, compass, and triangle for accuracy. Make the shape several inches in size. Using full inches for the measurements will make the next step easier.
3. For a pie-shaped grid, use the ruler or compass to mark off even measurements around the sides of the square or circle. With the ruler, connect these measured marks to make a pie-shaped grid. If you wish to use a square grid inside a circle, begin by constructing a grid of thirty-six squares. Place your compass point exactly in the center and adjust the radius to fit the square. Draw the circle.

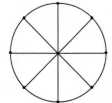 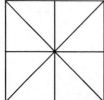 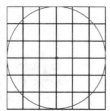

4. Begin at the edges by drawing shapes on the grid. Repeat the same shape in each section of the grid all around the edge. Shapes may cover more than one section and may reach in toward the center of the square or circle.

5. Continue to work toward the center of the circle or square. If the design gets too complex and confusing, erase some parts of it to make larger shapes. Be sure to draw the same design in all the corresponding sections, though. If the shapes are too large, draw other shapes inside or across them to break up the area. Use both curved and straight lines. Designs may come from flowers or leaves as well as abstract shapes.

6. Use colored pencils to color in the shapes in your design. Remember that all similar shapes should be the same color or alternating colors to preserve the repetitive quality of the design. Press hard on the colored pencils to make a dense color. Different colors can be blended together by coloring lightly with the lighter of two colors, and then going over it with the darker color. A third coat with the lighter color helps blend the two together. You may wish to blend from a light to a dark shade of the same color.

7. Cut out around the edge of your design and mount it on colored or black construction paper for display.

Assessment
- Evaluate the designs for radial structure and color, effective color combinations, and consistent techniques of coloring.

Lesson two: Design based on rectangles

Materials needed
- white drawing paper, 9" × 12"
- rulers
- triangles
- pencils
- white vinyl erasers
- compasses
- calculators
- markers, colored pencils, or crayons
- copier (optional)

Objective
The students will do the following:
- Construct a specific rectangle and use it to build a design

Procedure (pp. 227-28)
1. Following your teacher's instructions, you will construct either a golden rectangle or a rectangle based on the square root of five. To construct a golden rectangle, use a ruler and triangle to construct a square of any size. Measure to find the center of the bottom side. Place the point of the compass on the center mark and adjust the radius so that it intersects a top corner of the square. Draw an arc down from that corner to a line that is extended from the side of the square where the compass point is. The point at which the arc intersects the line will be the corner of your rectangle. Draw the rectangle by extending the top side of the square and moving the end.

The Modern World

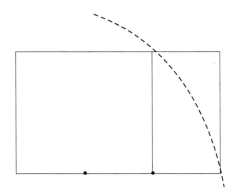

2. To construct a square-root-of-five rectangle, choose a length for the long side. Use millimeters for all your measuring to make the results more accurate. Divide that length by 2.236, the square root of five, to find the length of the shorter side. The resulting rectangle can be subdivided into five equal rectangles, which will all be square-root-of-five rectangles too.

3. The rectangle may be horizontal or vertical, or two or more may be combined into any shape. Experiment with the basic shape to find the most interesting combination possible.

4. Once you have your rectangular structure, you can organize anything you want into it. Still lifes, scenes, people, or abstract shapes can be used as long as they are organized by the rectangular structure. The lines of the rectangles do not have to appear on the picture, however.

5. Using markers, colored pencils, or crayons, plan your color scheme on the drawing. Perhaps you could make several photocopies to enable you to experiment with colors. Use colors that help draw attention toward your focal point and that reveal the rectangular structure.

Assessments
- Check the proportions of the students' rectangles to see if the students have organized the details of their drawings according to a rectangular structure.
- Assess the colors used for effectiveness in showing the focal point and for harmoniousness.

Lesson three: Painting
Materials needed
- rectangle drawings from Lesson two
- ballpoint pens
- rulers
- foam board, about 16" × 20", for each student
- pencils
- white vinyl erasers
- acrylic gesso
- 1½" inexpensive trim brushes or small trim paint rollers
- aprons, smocks, or old shirts
- acrylic paints (tubes of various colors plus one tube of white)

- nylon bristle brushes, various sizes
- Styrofoam plates for palettes

Objective
The students will do the following:
- Enlarge their designs and paint them with acrylic paints, choosing harmonious colors. Paintings may be flat and composed of abstract shapes, or they may be three-dimensional with modeled forms. They should show the same proportions and organization as the original drawings.

Procedure (p. 228)
1. Use a colored ink pen to draw an even grid of squares over your rectangle drawing. Be careful to measure accurately.

2. On a piece of foam board, measure the same number of squares as are on your rectangle drawing. The squares should fill the whole foam board and should be considerably larger than the squares on your drawing.

3. Working on one square at a time, transfer its contents into the larger square on the foam board, making light pencil lines. When all squares have been transferred, smooth the lines and erase any stray ones.

4. For best results, prime the foam board with acrylic gesso. It can be brushed on or thinned and rolled on with a paint roller. Use a disposable roller since the acrylic, if it dries in the roller, cannot be washed out. Wear an apron or smock to protect your clothes while you work with the gesso. When the gesso is dry, the lines will still be visible through it. If the foam board curls, paint the back also to straighten it.

5. Mix the colors of acrylic you want to use and begin to paint the areas of your painting. Acrylic is fairly transparent, so you cannot cover a dark color with a light one. Paint within your lines. Acrylic dries quickly; modeling must be done right away while the paint is still wet.

Note: Acrylic paints are water soluble only while they are wet. Once they dry, they cannot be washed out. Therefore, brushes must be washed out before they dry. Paint that spatters onto clothes should be washed out immediately. For this reason an apron or smock is recommended.

Assessments
- Have each student present his painting to the class along with the planning drawing, explaining what he did and why.
- Evaluate the paintings for following the original planning drawings, the composition, and the students' creative and harmonious use of color.

Chapter 19: Gallery of Living Artists

Questions and Answers

Carl Blair

1. What does the title of this painting suggest to you? Explain your opinion by referring to specific details in the painting. *(Students' answers will vary.)*

2. Lay a piece of tracing paper over the reproduction. Ignoring the natural content, search for and trace the abstract shapes you see. How does the resulting design differ from the painting? *(The design is more mathematical, bolder, more abstract.)*

Emery Bopp

3. Think about how the artist has represented Francis Schaeffer's ideas. Schaeffer sees the danger in the world's way of dividing experience into separate spheres. How does Bopp interpret this danger? *(His symbolism visualizes this concept; the lower section, the temporal, will take over the upper portion, the spiritual.)*

4. What solution does the artist propose? Explain the solution using the imagery chosen by the artist. *(The blood of Christ in the chalice unifies the two sections of the painting—the spiritual and the temporal parts of life.)*

Leonard Piha

5. Explain the body's position and what it might mean to the artist. Does it seem to represent atonement for sin? *(The hands and head hanging down seem to express discouragement—not suffering anything like a crucifixion. It also seems more personal—unaware of anyone else.)*

Lesa Dodd

6. What do you think is the significance of these objects in Dodd's painting? What is their relationship to each other, and what does the Scripture in Mark tell us to do? *(She has included these objects to show that the prophecy is nearing its fulfillment. Mark tells us to be alert so that we are prepared.)*

Karen Brinson

7. What has this artist done so as to take some very traditional ideas and change them into a modern, personal statement? *(She uses the traditional shapes but makes them with new materials and combinations of materials. She makes frames out of new materials.)*

Kathy Bell

8. Note the number of different alphabet faces and sizes that have been used for the various parts of the message. What relationship do these have to the particular passage? *(Large letters communicate the central message from the Old Testament; smaller letters express passages that complete or demonstrate the original prophecy; red letters are a traditional way of giving a warning.)*

9. Does the work as a whole have an effect of peacefulness? If not, what effect does it have? *(Students' answers will vary; however, they should be able to explain their answers.)*

Sandra Bowden

10. Notice that her way of working is mathematical. She has measured and placed all the elements on the paper with lines that are left as part of the work. Why do you think she has done that? *(Perhaps she has done so to remind us that the Word of God is very orderly and that He planned His Word carefully.)*

Chris Stoffel Overvoorde

11. Can you see areas where texture serves these functions? *(They show the texture of the king's hair, beard, and hands. They show the shadows under the sleeves and on the left side of the garment. Vertical lines of the buildings focus us on Solomon's face; the line of the pendant and cuffs of the sleeves draw our attention to the hands and to the balance scale.)*

12. What is Solomon holding in his hand? *(a balance scale)* Why do you think the artist portrayed him this way? *(It symbolizes justice because both sides of the scale are equal.)*

Studies of the Tabernacle: *Art for God's Glory*

In the study of the tabernacle in the Old Testament, we have an excellent opportunity to see God's aesthetic principles at work, "that this material dwelling-place of God might be a safe guide and real assistance in promoting fellowship with Heaven—that it might convey only right impressions of divine things, and form a suitable channel of communication between God and man—it must evidently be constructed so as to express God's ideas, not man's" ("The Tabernacle in Its General Structure," *ISBE*, p. 204). This aim was uniquely accomplished, for the form and specific details of the construction and decoration were given by God to Moses just as His Word was given (Exod. 25:8-9). Furthermore, the craftsman in charge of the project, Bezaleel, was filled with the Holy Spirit. What we are looking at, therefore, is not the art of man, but the art of God. Among the many lessons that can be learned from a study of the tabernacle is a lesson on the proper use of art for God's glory.

I. The Nature of God

1. Read Genesis 1:26-27. What does it tell us about ourselves? _____

   _____

   _____

2. In Genesis 1:29-30, God explains to Adam why He put so many plants in the Garden of Eden. What reason does He give? _____

   _____

   In Genesis. 2:9 He adds a different reason. What is it? _____

   _____

   _____

   What does this second reason show us about God?

   _____

   _____

   _____

   What does this knowledge about God show us about ourselves? _____

   _____

   _____

3. Read Psalm 19:1-4. What is the language that goes out to all the earth? _____

   _____

   According to this passage, this language has no words that can be heard. You can easily see this if you read the verse without the italicized words. It says, "No speech nor language; their voice is not heard."

4. In Psalm 8:3-4 we learn what the silent language of the heavens is teaching. What is it? _____

   _____

   _____

5. When God was giving the instructions for the building of the tabernacle and its furnishings, He instructed the seamstresses who sewed the garments for Aaron and his sons to put pomegranates and bells along the hem of the garment. He gave two reasons. What were they (Exod. 28:2, 40)? _____

   _____

   _____

6. What does the example of the lily in Matthew 6:28-30 show us about the beauty of things in nature? _____

   _____

   _____

   Even the tiny creatures that live in the deepest, remotest parts of the sea exhibit great beauty. Because men cannot travel to those depths, they must send machines down to photograph the animals that live there. Those organisms carry their own powerful floodlights to illuminate their world since no sunlight penetrates that far. They live in darkness, unseen by the human eye, yet they are very beautiful. For whom was their beauty created? _____

   _____

   _____

II. The Artist

1. Read Exodus 20:4-6. The first thing God says about art is negative. What is it that God is prohibiting in this commandment? _____

_____

Now read Exodus 25:10, 18-20. Which of the furnishings of the tabernacle is being described? _____

_____

What is to be placed on each side of it? _____

_____

From these verses what can we conclude about art?

_____

_____

Remember that the Israelites had lived for four hundred years in Egypt where they saw idols worshiped every day. Many of them were probably involved in idol worship themselves.

2. In Exodus 31:2-11 two men were chosen. What are their names? _____

How did God prepare them for their job? _____

_____

List the specific things they were going to do for God.

_____

_____

_____

_____

In Exodus 35:34 what else had God called them to do?

_____

_____

List the other workers who were to be filled with wisdom (v. 35). _____

_____

In Exodus 28:3 another group is mentioned. What were they to make? _____

_____

3. Proverbs 10:16 tells us what the result of our labors will be. Read Proverbs 31:13, 18-19, 21-22, 24. How is this lady a good example of labor that tends to life?

_____

_____

_____

_____

4. Ephesians 4:28 tells us another reason that we should labor. What is it? _____

_____

_____

Is the woman in Proverbs 31 an example of this also?

_____

5. Philippians 4:8-9 tells us to focus our thoughts on things that please the Lord. If our thoughts are right, our actions will be also. List all the words in this passage that describe what we must think about.

_____

_____

_____

_____

6. How will our artwork be judged before Christ someday? That depends on what we do and how we do it. Look at I Corinthians 3:12-15. Since the work is to be tested by fire, why should we want to be using gold or silver instead of wood, hay, or stubble? _____

_____

_____

_____

7. The gold, silver, wood, hay, and stubble are metaphors, words that stand for something else. What do you think might be the things God wants to see in a Christian artist? _____

_____

_____

_____

_____

_____

III. The Materials and Methods Used

1. In Exodus 35:5-9 Moses told the people what was needed in order to build the tabernacle. List the things they contributed. _____

   _____

   _____

   _____

   _____

2. Did they contribute enough (Exod. 36:5-6)? _____

   _____

3. Where did the former slaves get so much gold (Exod. 35:22 and 11:2-3)? _____

   _____

   _____

4. What is the "blue, and purple, and scarlet" that the people were to bring (Exod. 35:6, 25)? _____

   _____

   What is "goats' hair"? _____

   _____

   Did you know that cashmere, which is used to knit very soft sweaters, is made from the long wool of a goat?

The "badgers' skins" in verse 7 could be translated "seal skins" or "porpoise skins." These skins would make a waterproof covering. The "shittim wood" in the same verse is acacia wood. Acacia wood is available in that part of the world and is a very durable, hard wood that was used for building boats.

5. What kind of oil was going to be used for burning the lamps (Exod. 27:20)? _____

   _____

   Who brought the oil and spices (Exod. 35:27-28)?

   _____

   Why do you suppose *they* specifically were asked to bring these things? _____

   _____

   _____

6. What kinds of stones were brought for the ephod (Exod. 39:10-13)? _____

   _____

   _____

   _____

7. Why did the people give (Exod. 35:21-22)? _____

   _____

8. In chapters 35-39, several artistic processes are listed. What are they?

   (Exod. 35:25) _____

   _____

   (Exod. 35:33) _____

   _____

   (Exod. 35:35) _____

   _____

   (Exod. 36:34) _____

   _____

   (Exod. 37:13) _____

   _____

   (Exod. 37:17) _____

   _____

   (Exod. 37:29) _____

   _____

   (Exod. 39:1) _____

   _____

9. What did the engraver engrave (Exod. 39:6)? _____

   _____

10. What decoration was embroidered on the hem of the holy garments that were made for Aaron and his sons (Exod. 28:33)? _____

   _____

   _____

Pomegranates are red, not blue or purple. Many of the decorations in the tabernacle were nonrealistic. The *Zondervan Pictorial Encyclopedia* of the Bible states that pomegranates may symbolize the unity of God's Word composed of many separate parts. The inside of a pomegranate contains many small, sweet, berrylike fruits. The pomegranate was one of the fruits gathered by the spies to show the wonderful fruit that grew in Israel (Num. 13:23).

IV. The Tabernacle as a Symbol

1. What was the purpose of the tabernacle (Exod. 29:45-46)? _____

_____

_____

2. Where was the tabernacle to be located (Num. 1:53; 2:17)? (Check Num. 2:3, 10, or 18-25.) _____

_____

_____

3. In Hebrews 9:24, the Bible says the things in the Old Testament were "figures of the true" things in heaven. Each of the parts of the tabernacle is a picture of the truth of redemption. What objects were found in the outer court of the tabernacle (Exod. 40:6-8)? _____

_____

What was the bronze altar used for (Exod. 40:29)?

_____

_____

What is the meaning of this activity for us (Heb. 9:25-26)? _____

_____

_____

_____

What was the laver used for (Exod. 30:18-21)?

_____

_____

What does the washing of the priests mean to us (John 13:9-10)? _____

_____

_____

_____

The verses in Exodus 30 show Christians the seriousness of keeping their lives free from sin.

4. What furnishings were found inside the tabernacle but not in the holy of holies (Exod. 40:22-26)? _____

_____

_____

What was put on the table (Lev. 24:5-7)? _____

_____

_____

Why were there twelve? _____

_____

According to Leviticus 24:2-3, when was the lampstand burned? _____

_____

What does the light reveal (II Cor. 4:6)? _____

_____

What was the little altar used for (Exod. 30:7-8)?

_____

_____

According to Psalm 141:2, what does incense symbolize? _____

_____

5. Inside the tabernacle, behind the veil, there was only one object. What was it (Exod. 40:2-3)? _____

_____

What was the "mercy seat" (Exod. 25:22)? _____

_____

_____

What beings were sculpted on it (v. 19)? _____

_____

Where do these beings serve (Ezek. 10:19-20)?

_____

_____

Once a year, the high priest entered the holy of holies. What did he do there (Lev. 16:14-15)? _____

_____

_____

_____

What does the sacrifice of the high priest picture for us (Heb. 9:12)? _____

_____

_____

_____

6. Once the beautiful objects were finished and put into the tabernacle, what happened (Exod. 40:34-35, 38)?

_____

_____

How many people could enter the holy place of the tabernacle (Lev. 16:17)? _____

Could the ark of the covenant be seen? _____

Why (Lev. 16:11-13)? _____

_____

_____

Could it be seen when it was moved (Num. 4:15, 20)?

_____

_____

In Hebrews 9, God reveals the symbolism of the tabernacle: it is to show us how to worship God. First of all, our sin had to be paid for with a death (the bronze altar/the cross); then our daily sins must be cleansed (the laver/confession, I John 1:9). When we enter God's presence (the tabernacle), we want Him to remember us (the loaves of showbread), we need light to see His glory (the lampstand), and we must pray (the altar of incense). Only then can we appear in God's presence (before the mercy seat) and find "grace to help in time of need" (Heb. 4:16).

Bibliography

Caldecott, W. Shaw. "The Tabernacle." *International Standard Bible Encyclopedia*. 5 vols. Edited by James Orr. Grand Rapids, Mich.: William B. Eerdmans Publishing Co., 1939.

Moorehead, W. G. *The Tabernacle, The Priesthood, Sacrifices and Feasts of Ancient Israel*. Grand Rapids, Mich.: Kregel Publications, 1957.

Reviews: *The New American Painting*

Divide into groups and read the following excerpts from reviews of the international show *The New American Painting,* which traveled throughout Europe in 1958 and 1959. Newman was one of the artists featured. For each review, note whether the reviewer is favorable to the new art, unfavorable, or ambivalent. List on the chalkboard the specific characteristics the reviewer likes or dislikes about the work. Refer to a book that contains reproductions of several abstract expressionist works and compare the list to the reproductions. Try to understand why the reviewer said what he said. With which reviews do you agree or disagree? Why?

Unsigned *Le Phare*. Brussels, December 14, 1958

Let us say quite bluntly that this enormous sideshow is the most frightening demonstration of impotence that has ever been hawked around the world.

As for the paintings themselves, they far exceed the worst excesses imaginable as for indigence, mediocre imitativeness, and intellectual poverty. One can examine here with consternation inkspots measuring 2 yards by 2 ½; graffiti enlarged 10,000 times, where a crayon stroke becomes as thick as a rafter; vertical stripes 2½ yards wide separate areas 2 yards wide; soft rectangles, formless scribblings, childish collections of signs; enough to make our own abstract painters blush for shame, exposed henceforth to the most humiliating comparisons.

The seventeen Americans presented to us as the most representative of the new transatlantic painting have neither craft nor imagination. They are free, perhaps, but they are pathetic creatures who make poor use of their freedom. (Ross, pp. 285-86)

John Canaday, "The City and the New York School." 1960 (First published in the *New York Times,* May 22, 1960)

In the ebullience, the vitality, and the exuberance of its first youth the art of . . . abstract expressionism captured the common denominator of a city. But it did not begin to capture the common denominator of a nation; it is New York painting, not American painting. And even as New York painting, there is plenty of question as to whether it gives any order or meaning, as art should do, to the energy it expresses, or whether it has created only explosive fragments. That is my quarrel with even the best of it.

Perhaps abstract expressionism cannot mean anything because the vast welter of New York is in itself meaningless, an unhappy possibility. If so, then the quarrel is not with the artist's limitation but with our time and our city, of which abstract expressionism offers a complete and authentic expression. But it seems to me that the expression is no more complete and authentic than are fireworks as an expression of what the Fourth of July means.

Fireworks are wonderful to look at but I do not think that they offer a very profound experience, and I would not want the sky filled with them all night, year after year. Similarly I enjoy looking at abstract expressionist painting, but there is a limit to how much of it one can take, and I am tired of hearing that its skyrockets are cosmic manifestations.

New York is always called an exciting city, and so it is. But the things that make it exciting also make it monotonous if they are not tied to something deeper than surface movement and color. That is what I look for in abstract expressionist painting, and do not find, and that is why I find it monotonous. A fine place for a visit, but I wouldn't want to live there (without the sustenance of those inner human values that are universal—even to New Yorkers—yet are non-existent in the painting of the New York School). (Ross, pp. 272-73)

Alan Clutton Brock. *The Listener.* London, March 19, 1959

To get the feel of this work it is necessary to see a large collection of it, like this, and for the paintings to be of the largest size, as here they certainly are. Given this, the direct effect on the senses is undeniable and even impressive; also the huge and heavy blots, the intricate webs of trickling colour; the violent slashes of black across white exert something like a spell and seem like magical signs which even if they cannot be interpreted still have power over the imagination. . . . There is an admirable richness and sometimes an extreme refinement of texture. It is not easy to understand why such pictorial qualities, which are usually associated with a long tradition of expert painting, should suddenly appear in America as if released by these completely uninhibited exercises with the brush; but it certainly is so, and most European work in this style would look tame beside the maniacal flourishes of these newly liberated giants. (Ross, pp. 291-92)

Marco Valsecchi, *Il Giorno*. Milan, June 10, 1958

I must say that American art derives from European art and is still sensitive to its cultural echoes, but nevertheless its character is so well defined, the images are so abundant and so permeated by the fantasy and motivations of Americans ideals, that one must admit it has by now the look of independence, decisively recognizable. . . . Their creative talent is more free because they are not bound to traditions, to deep-rooted cultures, as our artists are. Therefore the American artists succeed in reaching a greater freedom, with results more pleasant, vibrant, and cheerful. We have been told that they were wild: we find instead a festive pictorial quality without dramatic shocks. (Ross, pp. 279-80)

From Ross, Clifford, ed. and introduction. *Abstract Expressionism: Creators and Critics, An Anthology.* New York: Harry N. Abrams, 1990.

Resources

1. Crystal Productions, Box 2159, Glenview, IL 60025-6159. T: 1-800-255-8629, E-mail: custserv@crystalproductions.com.
2. Davis Publications, Inc., 50 Portland St., P.O. Box 15015, Worcester, MA 01608-9959. T: 1-800-533-2847.
3. Dick Blick Art Materials, P.O. Box 1267, Galesburg, IL 61402-1267. T: 1-800-447-8192.
4. Metropolitan Museum of Art, 255 Gracie Station, New York, NY 10028-0198.
5. Museum of Fine Arts, Boston, P.O. Box 244, Avon, MA 02322-0244.
6. Museum of Modern Art, 11 W 53 St., New York, NY 10019-5401.
7. NASCO Arts & Crafts. Tools, materials, and visual aids for teaching art at all levels. 901 Janesville Ave., Fort Atkinson, WI 53538-0901. T: 920-563-2446, F: 920-563-8296, 1-800-558-9595.
8. National Gallery of Art, Publications Service, Washington, DC 20565.
9. Reading & O'Reilly, Inc. Art visuals, full-color prints, art appreciation videos. P.O. Box 302, Wilton, CT 06897. T: 203-762-2854, F: 203-762-8295.
10. Sax Arts & Crafts. Tools, materials, and visual aids for teaching art at all levels. P.O. Box 2002, Milwaukee, WI 53201. T: 414-272-4900.
11. School Specialty, Chaselle Division, Arts & Crafts Catalog, 609 Silver St., Agawam, MA 01001. T: 1-800-242-7355.
12. Shorewood Fine Art Reproductions, Inc., 27 Glen Rd., Sandy Hook, CT 06482. T: 203-426-8100.
13. ShowForth, Bob Jones University Press. Greenville, SC 29614-0001. T:1-800-845-5731. Videos on the BJU Museum and Gallery, Inc. narrated by Dr. Bob Jones.
14. Triarco Arts & Crafts, Inc., 14650 28th Ave. North, Plymouth, MN 55447. T: 1-800-328-3360, F: 612-559-2215.

Visual Aids

1. *American Artists Reflect American History.* S & S, P.O. Box 513, Colchester, CT 06415-0513. T: 1-800-243-9232. Five books containing five posters each, 22" × 17", on various periods of American history. Includes a profile of the artist, information about the historical event, and a formal analysis of the painting.
2. *American Art Quiz.* Lifetime Books & Gifts, #SAF-1885. Card game in quiz format stored in plastic box.
3. Art Concepts Time Line. NASCO, Crystal Productions. Shows how art concepts have been used. Also includes music, architecture, religion, and historical events. Ten 19" × 26" panels make 22' in all.
4. Art History Timeline. Reading & O'Reilly, NASCO, Crystal Productions, Blick. 30' length printed on 27" × 13" panels. Each panel contains color reproductions plus background information for five centuries.
5. Create-A-Time-Line. NASCO, Crystal Productions, Blick. Allows you to create a personalized time line that can be removed and reorganized each year. The 27" × 13" panels combine to make more than 13'.
6. Elements of Design and Principles of Design. Crystal Productions. Available as two separate sets from School Specialty. Set of fourteen posters, 17" × 22" laminated surface with one large art reproduction and several small ones, plus description explaining each of the elements and principles of art.
7. Fabulous 40—Fine Art Prints. Reading & O'Reilly, Inc. Forty 22" × 17" coated prints with lesson guide, all levels.
8. *The Gallery Game, The Thinker's Guessing Game, The Thinker,* and *The Scribe.* Detroit Institute of Arts Museum Shop, 5200 Woodward Ave., Detroit, MI 48202. Art appreciation games.
9. Know the Artist Posters, and Drawing and Watercolor Posters. Crystal Productions. The large 17" × 22" posters explain and demonstrate how to draw and how to paint with watercolor. Eight or ten posters in each set.
10. *NASCO Art Question Quest.* NASCO. Uses a TV game show format with art questions in six categories. Enough questions included to play five games without repeating questions. Two to six players or teams.
11. Poster sets containing various numbers of poster-sized reproductions in each set. NASCO. All contain historical information about the artist and artwork. Sizes range from 12" × 13" to 19" × 24".
12. *The Shorewood Collections.* Full-color reproductions. Also *Art Reference Guide.* ISBN 088185-026-8. Also *Artists' Biographies for the Art Reference Guide.* Shorewood Fine Art Reproductions, Inc., Crystal Productions, NASCO.
13. Take 5 Art Prints. Crystal Productions. A series of five prints grouped by theme. Large 18" × 24" size with information about the artist, the artwork, and interpretations and critiques. Also includes teacher's guide.

Videos

Most of these are secular programs and should be previewed.

1. *The African American Experience.* Media for the Arts, 360 Thames St., Newport, RI 02840. T: 1-800-554-6008, F: 401-846-6580. Seven videos about African American artists, about 30 minutes each.

2. *Elements of Design, Principles of Design.* Crystal Productions. Include examples of each element or principle in art and in nature. Can be used together with the Elements and Principles posters above. Helps teach and reinforce concepts. 28 minutes each.

3. *Hearts and Hands.* L. Reese and M. Dougherty. Hearts and Hands Media Arts, 372 Frederick, San Francisco, CA 94117. Two videos explore nineteenth- and twentieth-century history through the medium of quilting. Comes with an educator's guide.

4. *Indian Pottery of San Ildefonso-Maria.* Weiner Video, Prod. no. VFH055. T: 1-800-622-2675. The work of Maria Martinez in traditional Indian pottery-making. 27 minutes.

5. *Media for Art Education.* National Archives and Records Administration, National Audiovisual Center, 8700 Edgewood Dr., Capitol Heights, MD 20743-3701. T: 301-763-1896 or, for credit card orders only, 1-800-638-1300. Series of video or films on art from the nation's galleries. Rentals and previews available.

6. *Pen Calligraphy.* Fran Strom. Weiner Video, Prod. no. VAC-14. T: 1-800-622-2675. Home-study course for beginners and intermediates. 88 minutes.

7. *Symbols in Religious Art,* #071142; *The Mannerists: Sixteenth-Century European Art,* #071118; *Splendors of Baroque: Italian Painting,* #02541; ShowForth. Guided tours of the famous BJU Museum and Gallery, Inc. hosted by Dr. Bob Jones. 29 minutes each.

8. *Wilton Art Appreciation Series.* Reading & O'Reilly, Inc. 300 level, for middle and secondary level, video and teacher's lesson book. 30-day free trial available.

Computer Software/CD ROM

These are secular programs and should be previewed.

1. *The Art Historian,* vols. 1 and 2. Davis Publications, Inc. Spans art history from ancient times to the present with multimedia lectures, archives, and ability to assemble collections for study as well as an interactive test to assess students' knowledge. CD ROM is Mac and Windows compatible.

2. *Art Rageous.* SoftKey International, Inc. 1 Athenaeum Street, Cambridge, MA 02142; Shareware Source, P.O. Box 925, Greenville, SC 29602. T: 864-232-7102, E-mail: sharsource@aol.com. A hands-on exploration of art elements with interactive games and art history. CD ROM is Mac and Windows compatible.

3. *Leonardo the Inventor.* Future Vision Multimedia, 300 Airport Executive Park, Nanuet, NY 10977. ISBN 1-57213-009-1. CD ROM is Mac and Windows compatible.

4. *Masterworks of Japanese Painting.* MAC #50556, MPC #2-50556, Educorp. T: 619-536-9999. CD ROM drawn from the largest private collection of Edo period Japanese art outside Japan.

5. *World of Art.* Great Christian Books, Prod. no. 05EDI-GEOSAFA37. Electronic Learning Game Pack explores the history of art and architecture with games. Ages 8-adult.

Additional Reading

Most of these are secular books and should be previewed.

1. *Addicted to Mediocrity.* Francis Schaeffer. Lifetime Books and Gifts, 3900 Chalet Suzanne Dr., Lake Wales, FL 33853-7763. T: 1-800-377-0390. #III-0017.

2. *Bible and Its Painters.* Bernard. Lifetime Books and Gifts, 3900 Chalet Suzanne Dr., Lake Wales, FL 33853-7763. T: 1-800-377-0390. #RAN-0023. The Bible illustrated by paintings, including the apocrypha.

3. *Christmas Story: Told Through Paintings from the Metropolitan Museum of Art.* Mühlberger. Lifetime Books and Gifts, #III-0030. New York: Gulliver Books, Harcourt Brace Jovanovich. ISBN 0-15-200426-2. Contains the text from the King James Bible as well as information about the artwork.

4. *Eyewitness Art: Essential Visual Guides.* Crystal Productions. New York: Dorling Kindersley. Series of large books about various art movements. Beautifully illustrated with a wealth of information. Six titles.

5. *Glorious Impossible.* Madeleine L'Engle. Lifetime Books and Gifts, #III-0107. The life of Jesus illustrated by frescoes of Giotto.

6. *The Masters of Art.* Crystal Productions. Ten large 10.5" × 14" books include color reproductions, explanations of techniques and materials, and biographical information. Hardcover.

7. *Talking with Artists.* P. Cummings. New York: Bradbury Press, 1992. ISBN 0-02-724245-5 Conversations with fourteen different illustrators whose work is included in the book.

8. *A Theology of Artistic Sensibilities: The Visual Arts and the Church.* J. Dillenburger, Crossroads Publishing Co., 1986.

Publication

Scholastic Art. Scholastic Inc., 730 Broadway, New York, NY 10003-9538, ISSN 0004-3052. Six issues per year, each featuring an artist with reproductions of his work and a sample lesson developed from his work.